Ripples
Groupwork in different settings

edited by

Oded Manor

Whiting & Birch

MM

© Whiting & Birch 2000

Published & distributed by Whiting & Birch Ltd, PO Box 872, London SE23 3HL, England.

Distributor USA: Paul & Co, Publishers' Consortium Inc, PO Box 442, Concord, MA 01742.

British Library Cataloguing in Publication Data.
A CIP catalogue record is available from the British Library

ISBN 1 86177 034 0 (limp)

Printed in England by Intype

The chapters in this book first appeared in *Groupwork* 11(3) and 12(1)

Contents

GROUPS ADDRESSING SOCIAL CONCERNS

Introduction

What is groupwork? The answer may depend on the person you ask.

So groupwork is whatever groupworkers say it is? Not quite: further reflection suggests that the setting in which workers practice determines many of the differences. In turn, the influence of the workplace on practice is not a matter of chance.

Groupwork is offered in different settings: hospitals, schools, community centres, social work agencies or private training institutions. Each of these is organised to meet somewhat different needs: concerns related to physical injuries, treated in hospitals, are not the same as the maturational needs of adolescents attending schools. The involvement of social workers in the safety and care of young children stems from needs that are different from those which preoccupy trainees in counselling and psychotherapy.

This diversity of needs leads to marked difference in practice, and so it should. The only danger lies in what I call 'the Columbus Syndrome': every time a new need is identified workers may imagine that they must discover a new continent: a totally different form of groupwork has to be invented - from scratch. Such bursts of creativity can be exciting yet also debilitating. Ignoring previous knowledge can lead to the neglect of important needs of group members. At worst, workers may be involved in exacerbating group members' situations.

A more disciplined brand of creativity can prevent the Columbus Syndrome. Surely, it is only sensible to first check what is already known about effective groupwork - from research and from practice. Then, of course each worker can introduce changes that meet the specific needs of group members within their own work-setting.

The purpose of this book is to point to as many different sources of groupwork knowledge as possible. Eleven contributions were invited. Hopefully, the obvious diversity does not obscure the underlying common ground. Indeed - you will see that, at times, the same sources are quoted in different chapters. In addition, I would suggest that three underlying currents can be identified in each application: process, structure and worldviews. In this context:

- *Processes* are the spontaneous moment-to-moment exchanges we share with people.
- *Structures* emerge when we repeat processes until a pattern of interaction is established.
- *Worldviews* contain the moral judgements we make while relating to other people.

Because these phenomena are well known the term 'group dynamics' is often used to refer to the ways these combine in each group. It is true that these underlying currents are not always made explicit. Yet, invariably the dynamics create certain ripples in each and every group.

Group dynamics appear in many guises - as many different combinations of process, structure and worldviews. Inevitably, the ripples that these combinations create will vary in each setting. The competent groupworker will be sufficiently familiar with the variety of influences of group dynamics to prevent obvious pitfalls. Such a worker will then be able to facilitate the ripples that best meet the needs of the members who joined the group—be they clients, users, students or patients. Such a worker will be able to select the aspects of group dynamics that are most relevant to the people involved as well as being manageable within each work-setting, and then apply these creatively.

To enhance such competence leading groupworkers were invited to introduce major applications of groupwork as practised in very different work-settings in Britain. Each author was asked the same set of questions:

- Who is involved - what are the particular needs of group members?
- How are people involved in this type of groupwork - the methods applied.
- The setting in which this form of groupwork is practised.
- Possible future developments of groupwork in this area.
- Leading texts where more details can be found.

Sharing many forms of practice with you involves ordering the contributions in some fashion. Simply to help you find your way, the main level of group members' involvement was used to cluster the eleven contributions into three sections:

- *Groups with a personal orientation*, where differences among individuals; for example, of temperament, personal history, a particular need, or a certain life style are very important.

- *Groups with an interpersonal focus,* where the roles people occupy; for example those of parents, of secondary school pupils, or of offenders, are central.

- *Groups addressing social concerns*, where the needs and aspirations which people share, over and above the differences among them, are pursued. Examples of these concerns might include continuous education, civil rights or control over resources.

A great deal of overlap exists among these three levels, and groupwork practice often reflects this overlap. Yet, the major goals of group members usually direct the workers to emphasise one of the levels more than the other two.

This book begins with groups that emphasise the personal level, moves on to groups that stress interpersonal issues and ends with those that address mainly social concerns.

Groups with a personal orientation

Personal growth groups are discussed by John Rowan in the first chapter. Rowan characterises these groups as aiming to 'bridge the big gap'. The gap that Rowan has in mind is between living according to the expectations others have of us, and our own vision of the ways each of us can be with other people: in intimate relationships, at work, and in socially organised situations. Personal growth groups are often offered during the training of counsellors and psychotherapists, but other educational institutions draw on these too. The personal level is vital in such groups, where spontaneous processes are often strongly emphasised.

Pam Firth's chapter on groupwork in palliative care stays at the personal level. Death and dying defy words though a young person can help us with an image, for example: 'When someone dies it's like a glass shattering'. Firth looks at various forms of helping the dying, and assisting the bereaved to 'pick up the pieces'. Firth also helps us understand the importance of working with those professionals who work with the bereaved. You will see that some of these groups elicit spontaneous processes, while others rely on organising discussion within a structure that meets the educational needs of their members. The hospice movement has contributed a great deal to this application of groupwork.

Groupwork in occupational therapy is introduced in Linda Finlay's chapter. This contribution is also a timely reminder that groupwork is not necessarily confined to sitting around and talking. Social groupwork has a long tradition of resorting to activities rather than merely talk, and these applications involve a skilled use of the group's structure. Finlay's emphasis on the value of activities in medical settings is vitally important if groupwork is to reach more people with increasingly diverse needs.

Groups with an interpersonal focus

In the criminal justice system groupwork focuses on the behaviours of group members that constitute the offence they committed. When a person is convicted of an offence that person enters a certain role – that of an 'offender'. Liz Dixon offers an extensive review of groupwork applications that address this interpersonal role. Highly structured approaches to groupwork are currently required by management in the criminal justice system. Dixon accounts for these and also raises crucial questions. For change rather than mere punishment to occur, offenders and people working with them have to feel personally involved in the change effort – they have to own their involvement in groupwork. Such ownership can evolve only when spontaneous processes are enabled too. Does the present trend towards evidence-based practice address the need for ownership?

Social work has seen the flowering of groupwork in the seventies and its near withering in the eighties. The chapter by Mark Doel and Catherine Sawdon shows that all is not lost. When a social work agency commits itself to encouraging practice through a training programme, groupwork can be revived. The range includes structured as well as free flowing process-oriented approaches to groupwork. The authors remind us that no group is an island: understanding the relevant organisational support is as crucial as the micro skills required for working with each group.

Groupwork in Mental health is reviewed in the following chapter. Many settings are involved: inside mental hospitals, in residential settings, in day centres and in the open community. The range of groupwork applications in mental health is very wide indeed, and I have tried to show how this range can be mapped out when mutual aid among group members is seen as the connecting thread.

However, health is an even wider issue than mental health. Ellen Reverand and Louis Levi recognise the broad remit implied in health promotion. The authors' account is of a front line groupwork project designed to develop the ability of professionals to help people expand their options. In their practice you can see an imaginative blend of structured and improvised approaches to groupwork.

Groups addressing social concerns

The concept of 'citizenship' is now a vital aspect of the National Curriculum taught in schools. Yet, Marion Silverlock takes us out of the classroom and into the community. Out there, where they live, youngsters learn to be citizens by designing and managing group projects that meet their own aspirations. Silverlock does not merely describe these recent innovations, but explores the importance of groupwork knowledge for the adults who enable the youngsters to learn in these new ways. A training programme for the facilitators is included.

Is learning confined to the young? Surely not. 'Life long learning' is now recognised as important to people of all ages. Lynne Muir takes up this theme to highlight recent developments outside formal institutions. Adults continue to learn vocational, recreational, artistic and even entrepreneurial skills, and they do so by devising their own curriculum in groups. Muir reviews various models that have shaped the current understanding of 'community based learning' and clearly identifies the contribution of groupwork knowledge, of structure as well as process, to opening up new possibilities for adults of all ages.

Community development can overlap with some social work practice. Jacky Drysdale and Rod Purcell show how community development groups address the current concerns about including marginalised people in mainstream social life: 'breaking the culture of silence'. At the same time, Drysdale and Purcell are able to underpin their work by one very well established model of group development where spontaneous processes are paramount, and, by doing so, demonstrate the connection between mainstream groupwork and community development.

Social action concludes this book. Aimed particularly at disempowered groups, social action tends to begin when the moral values that motivate action are clarified. Although not always declared, such a clarification relies on an active and skilful use of group structure. Using a rather broad canvass, Mark Harrison and Dave Ward paint a rich picture of the widely spreading applications of this distinct model.

Within this model values are the context of practice, and collective power is a major vehicle for realising these values.

*

By the time you reach the end of this book you may be driven in one of two directions. You may feel the need to choose one approach and apply it exclusively in your practice. On the other hand, you may reach the conclusion that, as workers practice in so many different ways, everything and anything goes - you may do whatever you fancy.

As mentioned in the beginning, I hope that you will not fall for either of these understandable yet simplistic views.

Careful reading of the texts shows that each approach is a particular blend of structuring relationships, and also enabling spontaneous processes to flow. Yet, the blend chosen for each group is not a matter of chance, fashion, or fancy.

In every human relationship process and structure are two sides of the same coin; one cannot be conceived without the other. The blend of these universal aspects of human relationships should be chosen with a certain purpose in your mind.

The chosen combination should help group members to achieve identified goals on which they, their workers and their agency have agreed. Yet mechanical listing of goals may well not be enough. This is because some goals are clusters of diverse and, at times, conflicting smaller goals. In addition, other goals keep changing as group relationships develop.

Therefore, it is vital to remember that the groupwork we are talking about here is grounded in certain moral values. Honesty with group members, dignity of the individual, meaningful working alliances, demystifying power and sharing it, promoting the value of diverse cultures, upholding the contributions made by minorities—these are some of the moral values that have guided groupwork practice for decades. Whether they write about it explicitly or not, the people who contributed chapters to this book certainly believe and practice according to these values.

As already suggested, worldviews and the moral judgements embedded in them, combine with process and structure to yield the group's dynamics. The ripples created by each group's dynamics will vary. Yet, as long as each worker is mindful of our shared source, the group's dynamics, and can account for the ways it is manifest in practice, many possibilities can evolve.

Elsewhere (Manor, 2000) I have gone into far more details about sustaining such a stance. The message I see emerging from this book is rather simple.

Let us keep innovating. Groupwork is a deep, rich resource that can be applied to meet many different needs in a wide range of settings. As we do so, let us also learn more from one another. To do so we shall need to understand each other more clearly. One way of furthering such understanding is to always attend to each group's dynamics. Then the universal aspects of group dynamics can become our shared language.

Groupwork practice is creative, constantly changing, and very diverse. I hope that this panoramic view of groupwork applications will serve to enhance informed dialogues among practitioners from many different disciplines who work in a wide range of settings. Further development of groupwork depends on interdisciplinary collaboration, and such collaboration can be firmed up when more practitioners monitor their practice, explain what they do and write it up so that others can learn from their experiences.

The journal *Groupwork* was created to facilitate such mutual learning. Indeed, in recent years, deliberate steps were taken to expand the range of professions represented in the editorial board so that mutual learning expands further. This book is an example of the current collaboration that began in the special issues 'Groupwork across the Disciplines'.

We hope that you will join our readers, and that you too will send *Groupwork* your account of practice in your own setting.

Oded Manor
Editor

Reference

Manor, O. (2000) *Choosing a Groupwork Approach: An inclusive stance.* London: Jessica Kingsley.

Groups
with a personal orientation

Crossing the great gap:
Groupwork for personal growth

John Rowan

Groups for personal growth are explained as part of following Maslow's theory of a hierarchy of needs. Such groups can be either voluntary or part of required training. In neither case does the participant have to be sick or suffering, and two main forms of growth groups can be identified: the humanistic and the psychodynamic. The classic and original growth groups were humanistic, and their purpose was to enable the participant to become a whole person, to become self-actualized. The process involved crossing the gap between getting esteem from others and giving it to ourselves. That emphasis on humanistic values such as autonomy and authenticity has continued. Currently, all work in groups is concerned with trust, safety and confrontation. Some of the questions that arise, such as whether such groups should be required for training in counselling and in psychotherapy, are then discussed and also their political significance. Comments about the future of personal growth groups concludes this chapter.

Introduction

Personal growth is a term coming from humanistic psychology (Rowan, 1988). This approach has many forms: person-centred therapy, Gestalt therapy, psychodrama, bioenergetics, focusing, experiential therapy, existential analysis and some of the feminist and transpersonal methods. In this context, growth strictly means development in terms of the Maslow (1987) theory of a hierarchy of needs. This theory says that we all start off with physiological needs. When these are satisfied, we move on to safety needs, involving basic trust. When these are satisfied, we can move on to the higher levels as we grow up; for example, learning our roles so as to be good conformists. As Kohlberg (1981) showed through his research, we can then continue growing, and so move from the conventional to the postconventional forms of consciousness.

Group work is particularly good for moving across what I have called 'the Great Gap'. This is the gap between levels 4 and 5 (Rowan, 1988, pp.8-9) of Maslow's hierarchy. This gap is between needing esteem from others, and looking to them to see how they expect us to behave, and moving on to giving esteem to ourselves and being open to discovering what each of us can be. Crossing the great gap begins when the group gives us a forum for questioning our customary assumptions and our usual roles. Being real is central in personal growth groups. Being real simply means not hiding behind our roles and the expectations we have adopted without noticing: our unaware 'shoulds'. In personal growth groups we say what we mean and mean what we say. We see out of our own eyes, rather than out of the eyes of others. We take full responsibility for what we say and do. Learning how to do this is often harder than we thought at first it would be, and group work is ideally suited to help in this. The group works by confronting us with the task, and supporting us in carrying it out. This combination of support and confrontation is crucial to group work, as Peter Smith's (1973) work has shown.

Two kinds of personal growth groups

There are really two main kinds of personal growth groups, in terms of the people who go to them. Firstly there are groups which people go to entirely off their own initiative, for their own satisfaction. Very often the impetus is a crisis of some kind. Perhaps their partner has left them, or perhaps they have lost their job, or perhaps a child has died, or perhaps it is just something much more minor, but worrying enough to lead them into a re-examination of their life.

That impetus can also be just curiosity and enterprise, looking into the possibilities open to them. This, too, can be very productive. 'Making the able more able' may be the slogan here. Many people have taken this risk, and gone to a group simply to clarify their feelings, learn more about themselves, and improve their personal lives. These groups can help to change both a person's understanding and acceptance of themselves, and also improve their ability to relate to other people.

Secondly there are the personal growth groups which are part of a course in counselling or psychotherapy. Here the person is required to go to the group to enhance the personal development that is expected to take place on such a course. It would not be right, the reasoning goes, to try to counsel other people if one had done no work on oneself. These groups are often a humbling experience, which demonstrate convincingly to people that they are not as ready to become counsellors as they had thought at first. In all cases those attending are not called 'patients' but rather 'participants' or 'group members'.

The people who lead such groups are counsellors or psychotherapists who have taken specific training in groupwork, and are experienced at working in this way. They are usually in supervision, but in privately run groups there is no guarantee of this. If this is a concern, it is easy enough to ask about it.

Not for sick people

The general point to be made about personal growth groups is that there is no assumption made in these that people are sick or inferior or defective in any way, as can be seen very easily in the Maslow model. Joining a group simply involves following a developmental path a bit further than most people bother to do. The journey begins with the permission and encouragement to be real. Then quite a number of specific approaches are mobilised in the search for further help in crossing the great gap.

Jacob Moreno (see Karp et al, 1998) was one of the pioneers of this direction. Through the method of psychodrama, which he developed, Moreno showed how people could be helped to be more creative and spontaneous than they had been before. In psychodrama people can re-enact scenes from their past with the help of other group members. Each member takes different roles; for example, that of their father, or mother, or a previous teacher. The member then acts as if they were that figure. Group members can also see themselves acted out by others. Each member can then change their current responses to others in their daily lives, or see other possibilities of getting out of old and apparently impossible situations.

Carl Rogers (see: Kirschenbaum & Henderson, 1990) was another pioneer, insisting that a growth group had to be person-centred in the sense of helping people to find who they really were instead of having fixed aims for them. People in person-centred groups are encouraged to give up the masks they generally use to get by in social interactions. Instead, each member is enabled and supported in expressing directly and genuinely the feelings that arise for them in the group. Rogers' emphasis on genuineness, empathy, and acceptance has influenced many other approaches to counselling and to psychotherapy.

A third name that must be mentioned is that of Fritz Perls (see Clarkson & Mackewn, 1993). Perls developed Gestalt therapy and emphasised awareness and personal presence. He insisted on paying attention to the how (rather than the why) and the now (rather than the past or future). Perls encouraged paying attention to unfinished cycles of making contact with people, and to the splits we create to disrupt such cycles. An example can be to apologise whenever the cycle would call for expressing anger. In this case the cycle of contact is disrupted by splitting the expression of anger from the expression of appreciation. He also developed ways of enabling group members to intensify the aspects they split; for example, expressing appreciation more intensely and then expressing anger more loudly. By shuttling between the two extremes, a new resolution emerges. Fritz Perls' contribution was important in regard to the theory of paradoxical change (Beisser 1972) that has been adopted in many other areas of counselling and of psychotherapy.

Whatever approach is followed, we all need help to begin crossing the gap. Up until the Great Gap, society gives a great deal of support and help in ascending the Maslovian hierarchy of needs. It may even sometimes feel like being carried up on an escalator. But at the point where the Great Gap begins, society ceases to encourage us, and we have to carry on by ourselves, under our own steam. We have to become more autonomous in order to progress at all. That is where these types of growth groups come in. In this sense there is a sort of paradox about growth groups: we join them to become more autonomous, yet we have to be a little bit autonomous in order to take the risk of joining such a group.

A range of types

Shaffer & Galinsky (1989) offer a very good account of the range of groups that have been developed over the years. They describe: the social work group; the psychoanalytic therapy group; the group-dynamic therapy group; the existential-experiential group; psychodrama; the gestalt therapy workshop; behaviour therapy in groups; the Tavistock approach to groups; T-Groups and the laboratory method; the encounter group; the theme-centred interactional method; and the self-help group. In each case they give a general introduction and historical background, an illustration of a typical session, key concepts and special techniques, and comments about the role of the leader.

Any of these groups can be used for personal growth, although this is not always the case. In practice the two main approaches in this country are the person-centred group developed by Carl Rogers in the USA, and naturalised into the UK by people like Brian Thorne, Dave Mearns and Tony Merry, and the group-analytic group developed by Sigmund Heinrich Foulkes in Britain. The person-centred group is most similar to the encounter group or the existential-experiential group as described by Shaffer & Galinsky, and comes from the humanistic camp. The group-analytic group is most similar to the group-dynamic group or the psychoanalytic group as described by Shaffer & Galinsky, and is often described as a psychodynamic group. There are other types of group on offer in some locations, such as psychodrama groups, which are in most cases excellent now, because the training has become quite rigorous in recent years. Gestalt groups are also now mostly run by well-trained people, and are a very good source for use in your own work on yourself. Tavistock groups are not so good for personal growth, and are of more use to people working in organisations who want to deal with their fantasies about authority figures.

We must not forget the self-help group. People who want to embark on a programme of self-development often find in self-help groups a way of doing the work they need to do without spending large sums of money. Sheila Ernst & Lucy Goodison (1981) have written an excellent text on this, which gives a great deal of information about starting up and running such a group. Co-counselling (Evison & Horobin, 1988) is a way of working in a one-to-one way, though groups are also used. A brief training course is involved, but after that the procedure is free. The women's movement developed a variety of consciousness-raising groups. The men's movement has included various forms of groups where men explore how to change and develop new gender identities and gender roles (Rowan, 1997).

Aiming at the whole person

Personal growth groups, in the sense of groups that did not assume any pathology, started in the 1960s as part of what was called the growth movement. They often took place in growth centres such as the Esalen Institute in California or the Open Centre in London, both of which still exist. The idea was that all the techniques used in psychotherapy, and new ones too, could also be used simply for the benefit of ordinary people with no particular illnesses or defects. Such people could then develop further, and leave behind their compulsions, unconsidered assumptions and unexamined values, and ascend the Maslovian ladder. They could grow to become what Carl Rogers used to call 'a fully-functioning person', or 'that self which I truly am' - what Maslow called the self-actualised person. Nowadays the number of growth centres has diminished, but the approach is more widespread than ever, forming part of virtually every course in counselling and psychotherapy. Counsellors and psychotherapists, more than most, need to be whole persons, as Jung (1966) pointed out long ago.

Some key issues

Generally speaking, psychodynamic groups have lower horizons, and have more restricted aims. They are more oriented toward adjustment and coping. But some of them, with a more eclectic approach, do seem a bit more ambitious. So far as personal growth in the psychodynamic group is concerned, one of the best discussions is to be found in the chapter by Wolf & Kutash (1986). They go into the interesting question, for example, of how things can go wrong in such groups.

Some of the important issues which arise in all personal growth groups are trust, safety and confrontation.

Trust

Trust influences learning, because we have to trust a message to some degree before we can even hear it, never mind learn from it. Trust influences cooperation, because it is hard to cooperate with someone if we do not trust them. Trust influences getting along with others, establishing friendships and inspiring the confidence of one's peers.

Trust is just as important in a group as it is in individual therapy, but it is actually harder to achieve. This experience is important in both cases because we cannot open up to another person if we do not trust them. Risking (very necessary in a good group) and trusting go hand in hand.

In a group, if no one takes any risks, stagnation can easily result. But mistrust can get in the way of risking anything. However, there is a paradox here. There is no way of proving that anyone is trustworthy: so we are always going to have to go beyond the evidence if we are going to get anywhere at all. If there is no way of ever proving finally that a person or group is trustworthy, we may as well take a risk and find out that way. So in order to engender trust, we have to act as if we trusted even if we do not trust. We have to risk if we are going to create trust. Then a two-way interaction can start up between trust and co-operation, and the whole group can come alive.

Trusting behaviour influences risk-taking: this is the basic point. To test whether someone is trustworthy involves taking some kind of risk. This testing goes on more at the beginning of a relationship than later on, but it can be renewed at any point where trust wavers. Perceived trustworthiness makes everything easier. Relying on the words or actions of another is never total, nor should it be, because that way lies disappointment and disillusion. But openness is certainly to be aimed at: partly because it is one of the goals of groupwork in terms of personal growth. In turn, openness means the owning of behaviour: taking responsibility for our own actions. The door to cooperation can only be opened from our side. We cannot expect someone else to do it for us.

Safety

Often at the beginning of a group people are a little scared of what might happen. The customary reassurance about confidentiality and prohibiting violence in the group do not go very far to allay their fears. But really the best answer to this is given by Starhawk (1987), when she says:

> Safety in a group is not a matter of niceness or politeness ... But a group can establish safety by assuring that risks are shared, that boundaries are clear, and that power structures and hidden agendas are brought out into the open. We cannot eliminate risks, but we can face them with solidarity. (Starhawk, 1987, p.145)

It is part of the role of the group leader to hold the boundaries of the group, and to ensure that important issues are not ignored or glossed over.

Confrontation

Confrontation (sometimes also called challenging) has to be well handled if it is to be fruitful. Confrontation is best done in the spirit of accurate empathy; really trying to get into the other person's shoes before speaking. It should be tentative rather than dogmatic. It should be done with care - there should be some real involvement with the other person. It should be done with attention to your own motivation: is it really for the other person's benefit, or for your own benefit? It is better to use real communication so that the message comes from your own self and your own experience, not from some pseudo objectivity. One handy slogan that emphasises real communication and how to achieve it is: 'Use giraffe language, not jackal language'. Giraffe language is always a description of what is happening inside you: it is a kind of owning up. The giraffe is the animal with the biggest heart in the jungle. Jackal language attacks the other person by labelling, by blaming, by questioning, by preaching - all types of communication which distance us from the other person and make them defensive.

Also important in a group is how you respond to confrontation: try not to be defensive. Let in the communication, and make sure you understand it. Ask questions if necessary to clarify what is being said, and listen to the answers.

Answers to questions

All these types of groups have been well researched, and the interested reader can find the key references in Shaffer & Galinsky. There is also some good material in Chapter 9 of Brammer, Abrego & Shostrom (1993) that goes into considerable detail, and gives many further references to follow up.

Questions have been raised about the value of groups like these in counselling training, for example by Irving & Williams (1996). Are these groups really necessary for good training? But good replies to the worries about this have come from Lyons (1997) and Mearns (1997). If the group can have the effect of enabling people to understand themselves better, and understand how they come across to other people better, and interact with other people more effectively, it can obviously help them to be better counsellors or psychotherapists. It seems that the personal growth group as a required part of training is not on its way out just yet.

Questions have also been raised about the politics of such groups. Yet, some of these groups have been very political (see: Ernst & Goodison, 1981) and have worked well in raising issues around feminism, sexuality, race and religious experience. Such issues are by no means ruled out in personal growth.

The future

This is a healthy and burgeoning field, and it is to be expected that such groups will continue for many years to come. Personal growth groups are grounded in a long tradition of philosophers concerned with existentialism. James Bugental (1981), who is both humanistic and existential, is one of the classic writers on the subject; particularly on authenticity: the drive to be real and fully present while being with people. In fact, there is a new interest in existentialism and phenomenology in universities at the moment (van Deurzen-Smith, 1997), and personal growth groups are oriented very much towards the values of such approaches. As already mentioned, one of the key concepts in existentialism is authenticity, and this is also one of the key values in humanistic psychology.

Genuineness and authenticity are still not talked about much in academic psychology, but in a personal growth group these values are often highly cherished. People express such values in the phrase - 'Say what you mean and mean what you say' - an expression that is all about authenticity, and one which is a major aim of personal growth groups. The experience of being authentic, fully alive and present, is close to the end of the path leading to self-actualization. As I said at the beginning, it is about seeing through your own eyes, instead of seeing the world through the eyes of other people. In a post-modern climate, it is salutary to remember that truth is still important, no matter how difficult it may be to reach it. To get in touch with our own inner truth is also important, and there is a great deal of research available to say that this task is a feasible one. We can know ourselves and we can relate to others.

Good sources on groupwork

Dayton, Tian (1994) *The Drama Within: Psychodrama and experiential therapy*. Deerfield Beach: Health Communications
This is a good thick book that covers both theory and practice. There is a specific chapter on working with addictions, alcoholism and the adult children of people addicted to alcoholic. Psychodrama is one of the basic humanistic disciplines, and it always offends me when books on group work leave out psychodrama. It is so flexible and useful, and can go so deep.

Ernst, Sheila and Goodison, Lucy (1981) *In Our Own Hands: A book of self-help therapy*. London: The Women's Press
This advertises itself as a book for women, but really it is for everyone. It contains full details about starting up and getting going, and many exercises to use with a full rationale. There is a lot of political awareness in it, and exercises on racism, sexism and so forth.

Houston, Gaie (1984) *The Red Book of Groups and How to Lead Them Better*. London: Rochester Foundation
What a delightful book this is! It breathes the spirit of humanistic psychotherapeutic approaches, and contains many valuable hints and tips for the aspiring leader. There is a lot of Gestalt in it, but it is not a purist book, just a very useful one. It has a lot of little cartoons in it too, which are humorous and pointed. Gaie also wrote another book called Being and Belonging (Wiley 1993) which takes the reader through a whole Gestalt group from beginning to end in a fictional fashion, and some people have found this illuminating.

Rowan, John (1992) Integrative encounter. in W. Dryden (ed) *Integrative and Eclectic Therapy: A handbook*. Buckingham: Open University Press
A spirited account of the full range of the encounter group, which is the most general kind of group in the humanistic camp. Gives a good sense of the issues it can cover.

Schutz, W. C. (1989) *Joy: Twenty years later*. Berkeley: Ten Speed Press
This is the original book from 1967, lightly updated. It is a classic book, full of the spirit of the pioneers, and containing much useful material. This is a masterwork, written by someone who has finally made his method part of himself. Schutz brought out a much more formal book (Schutz, W. 1973, Elements of Encounter . London: Joy Press) which is a superb brief rundown on the theory and practice of the open encounter group.

Shaffer, J. & Galinsky, M.D. (1989) *Models of Group Therapy* (2nd ed) Englewood Cliffs: Prentice-Hall
This is simply one of the best academic book on groups. It covers twelve types of group, and explains the rationale and procedures of each one. It is one of the very few academic books to do justice to the encounter group. They refer, for example to 'its important influence in helping to reduce the traditional distinction between a growth and development group on the one hand and a psychotherapy group on the other.' If you want a reference to use for your essay, this is the place to come.

Starhawk (1987) *Truth or dare: Encounters with power, authority and mystery* San Francisco: Harper & Row
You would never guess from the title that this is a book on group work, but in fact it is a very good one. It contains a lot of discussion of group processes and orientations, and also a number of very usable exercises, rituals and meditations. It is written by a feminist witch.

References

Beisser, A. (1972) The paradoxical theory of change. in J. Fagan & I.L. Shepherd (eds) *Gestalt Therapy Now*. New York: Harper

Brammer, L. M., Abrego, P. J and Shostrom, E. L. (1993) *Therapeutic Counselling and Psychotherapy*. (6th ed) Upper Saddle River: Prentice Hall

Bugental, J.F.T. (1981) *The Search for Authenticity. (Enlarged edition)* New York: Irvington

Clarkson, P. and Mackewn, J. (1993) *Fritz Perls*. London: Sage

Ernst, S. and Goodison, L. (1981) *In Our Own Hands: A handbook of self-help therapy* London: The Women's Press

Evison, R. and Horobin, R. (1988) Co-counselling. in J. Rowan & W. Dryden (eds) *Innovative Therapy in Britain.* Milton Keynes: Open University Press

Irving, J. and Williams, D. (1996) The role of group work in counselling training. *Counselling,* 7, 2, pp.137-139

Jung, C.G. (1966) Psychotherapy and a philosophy of life. in *Collected Works,* XVI, para 179. London: Routledge

Karp, M., Holmes, P. and Tauvon, K.B. (1998) *The Handbook of Psychodrama.* London: Routledge

Kohlberg, L. (1981) *The Philosophy of Moral Development.* San Francisco: Harper & Row

Lyons, A. (1997) The role of group work in counselling training. *Counselling* 8, 3, pp.211-215

Maslow, A.H. (1987) *Motivation and Personality.* (3rd ed) New York: Harper & Row

Mearns, D. (1997) Achieving the personal development dimension in professional counsellor training. *Counselling,* 8, 2, pp.113-120

Rowan, J. (1988) *Ordinary Ecstasy: Humanistic psychology in action* London: Routledge

Rowan, J. (1997) *Healing the Male Psyche: Therapy as initiation.* London: Routledge

Shaffer, J. & Galinsky, M.D. (1989) *Models of Group Therapy.* (2nd ed) Englewood Cliffs: Prentice Hall

Smith, P.B. (1973) *Groups Within Organizations.* London: Harper & Row

Starhawk (1987) *Truth or Dare: Encounters with power, authority and mystery.* San Francisco: Harper & Row

van Deurzen-Smith, E. (1997) *Everyday Mysteries: Existential dimensions of psychotherapy.* London: Routledge

Wolf, A. and Kutash, I.L. (1986) Psychoanalysis in groups. in I.L. Kutash & A. Wolf (eds) *Psychotherapist's Notebook.* San Francisco: Jossey-Bass

Picking up the Pieces:
Groupwork in Palliative Care

Pam Firth

The impact of a diagnosis of cancer on the patient and his family is immense and has far-reaching consequences; therefore, the needs of patients and their families have to be addressed at a number of levels. This chapter will explore two groupwork approaches to helping the patients help themselves, two that meet the needs of children whose parent(s) have died and a fifth that supports the staff working in this area. Such diversity of perspectives is crucial for understanding the relevance of groupwork to palliative care.

Hospice and specialist palliative care services aim to promote comprehensive care for people with progressive advanced diseases and a short life expectancy. The aims are to maximise the quality of life remaining, enabling patients to 'live until they die', and services include psychosocial care as well as adequate pain and symptom management. (National Council, 1997a). The term 'to palliate' means to cloak. The intention is to surround the person with conditions that ease their struggle with the disease. All aspects of living are included therefore, so that the holistic care offered caters to psychological, social, cultural and spiritual needs.

Groupwork was a popular social work activity in the seventies but recently it seems to have fallen out of use. Groups can be very effective in returning power and control to people who are particularly vulnerable, but there is a great deal of fear around groupwork in hospices, because talking about dying raises anxieties about contagion and increased distress. My experience in working with dying patients, carers and the bereaved leaves me confident that there are immense gains for the group members.

Dying and bereavement are lonely experiences in late twentieth century Britain, a society that is now highly organised and mobile. Families are smaller and often disconnected from their extended families and communities. Beliefs and rituals that help people in times of crisis are often lost. In this context, groupwork can help people counter the view that dying is a private, personal experience. Through discussion of individual feelings and apprehensions, death is no longer viewed as something 'out there', but an outcome that can be shared with others in the same boat.

Mutual support and collective problem solving can lead to groups examining their beliefs and devising new rituals. The creative forces that can be unleashed within groups of seriously ill people are unbounded. I shall illustrate this through four examples. The first is an open group for cancer patients.

The open group for cancer patients

The open group for cancer patients took place as part of a structured day programme, at a day hospice for younger people with cancer, most of whom had secondary diseases.

The group had to be open to allow for absences due to patients needing to attend hospital for treatment etc. The weekly one-hour sessions were facilitated by two social workers with up to sixteen members attending each time.

The structured day for younger cancer patients and carers was set up during the school term and the members were invited to come to a meeting to explore the idea of a discussion group. A room was chosen which would be suitable to hold the group and we began exploring and negotiating about the remit. Members were keen that the group should have a programme. This reflected anxiety that there might be too much dwelling on illness, symptoms, death and dying. However, a decision was subsequently made that some sessions should be left open so that members could use them as they wanted. Later, these free sessions were often used by members to bring poetry and prose they had written.

Members of this group clearly felt empowered by the experience of determining their own programme. The selection of speakers reflected their search to make sense of and manage their illness. Outside speakers comprised reflexologists, image consultants, beauticians, nutritionists, Chinese medicine practitioners, poets and a very popular base guitarist from an internationally famed sixties pop group. Members organised laughter workshops, quizzes and a games session, which coincided with half term, when smaller children joined us. Hospice staff were asked to give sessions and the Hospice physiotherapist was regularly asked to help them manage the physical manifestations of anxiety, as well as disabilities caused by the disease and treatment.

The group members then moved on to issues around their spiritual journey and the hospice chaplain was invited to attend. Subsequently, she arranged a regular fortnightly slot outside the group. Reflections about underlying fears and preoccupations found a place within the free sessions and time was left over, after presentations, for feelings which might have been stirred up, to be examined.

The group met for eighteen months before a group member died (Kraus, 1996) and this was followed by several more deaths in quick succession. Discussion about remembering the dead person revealed that acknowledging and saying goodbye to them could happen at several times during the day, e.g. news time, quiet time, relaxation etc. The group did not want to spend all their time remembering individuals, but needed some diversion as well as opportunities to talk about themselves, e.g., their death, their children's future and often the suddenness of death - how would they know when their time had come? It was important for group members to know they would be remembered. (Monroe, 1997).

The group was a very important part of a structured day care experience for people under fifty-five years of age who had cancer. This day care experience was named 'Genesis' by group members and accepted people who had a terminal diagnosis, as well as those undergoing active treatment. The small group programmed at the end of the day care became a place where important issues about the organisation of the day and discussions about future management ideas could be explained. The discussion group also contributed to the editing of the leaflet known as 'The Big C'.

Evaluation and reviews were carried out at the end of term. The programme for the next term was adjusted accordingly. Members' perception of the discussion group was that it did have benefits in making them feel less isolated. Staff worries that hearing the harrowing stories of other group members would disturb individuals did not seem to be borne out by experience. Members felt they were already 'as good as dead'; that they had died socially in the minds of others. (Charmez, 1980). One seventeen-year-old girl who attended the group for the six months before her death, reported that coming to the Day Hospice and attending the group gave her something to contribute in family discussions. This was at a time when she could not go out or do the 'normal things' expected of a seventeen-year-old.

Communication for these members was not only verbal; gestures and body language could all express so much. A randomised, controlled trial by Spiegel et al (1981) suggests that participation in support groups might prolong the survival of individuals with cancer. Many of the original members of this group are still alive, four years later.

Evaluation of the day provision for younger cancer patients has led to a change of service at the Day Hospice, which now offers a two-day programme. Younger patients now have a day programme of their own, which offers nursing input as well as some elements of the original provision described earlier. It has no discussion group but instead has a range of creative activities including art and creative writing. The second day is for patients who are at an early stage of their disease and this group was then offered a place in a psychoeducational programme, described next.

The psychoeducational group

In psychoeducational groups, patients are expected to attend ten sessions and most will then return to work. These groups aim to help people in the first stages of shock and fear following diagnosis. The emphasis is on self-help and managing the ambiguity of having a cancer diagnosis.

Each group is facilitated by two workers, but outside speakers give talks, demonstrations etc, for 30 minutes followed by discussion. The programme includes:

- cancer and its treatment, facts and questions;
- safe exercise and basic relaxation;
- Yoga;
- complementary therapies as a way of helping to manage your disease and the effects of treatment;
- spirituality;
- nutrition;
- mouth care;
- body image;
- session with a potter.

The potential power of this programme has been taken very seriously and safeguards have been built-in. All the team involved have taken part in a practice run, including role - playing patients and listening and commenting on the proposed presentations. The programme has been well supervised and intends to foster a culture of hopefulness and empowerment, without denying the fear and anxiety of members. Trijsburg et al (1992) found that nineteen out of twenty-two studies of psychosocial interventions for cancer patients in controlled trials, using a psychoeducational approach, produced positive effects; with none showing adverse consequences. They found some evidence that inclusion of training in coping skills or stress management conferred additional benefits.

Cunningham (1999) describes a brief psychoeducational programme for cancer patients and family members in a large group format. He assessed levels of stress before and after the course and found that there were improvements demonstrated both clinically and statistically. He found, as we found in our first groups, that interest was well maintained as shown by attendance figures. We did not feel that we would have the numbers to do this, nor did we feel confident about delivering a programme to a group larger than 20 members.

However, when a person is diagnosed as suffering from cancer everybody in the person's family is affected. This is why we also work with families of cancer patients, and my next example is of a group for bereaved children.

Group for bereaved children

Most of my work in palliative care settings has centred on young families and there are many examples of groupwork projects with bereaved children. Probably the best known is the Winston's Wish project, but we all owe much to the pioneering work of Sue Smith and Margaret Pennells. The essence and power of their work can be seen in two excellent videos 'That Morning I went to School' and 'Childhood Bereavement'.

Groups for bereaved children tend to be structured on a psychoeducational model. Staff running the CATS bereavement support programme for children and adults at Isabel Hospice, have modified the early work of Smith and Pennells (1995). The group now owes much of its development to the influence of art and drama therapies.

The staff at Isabel Hospice and East Herts. NHS Trust lead regular eight week sessions of activities which allow bereaved children to express their feelings and gain understanding through drawing, role playing, modelling, playing and talking.

Parents and carers attend with their children and participate in the programme concurrently, but in separate rooms. The investment in training staff and volunteers, in providing a safe environments and in ensuring on-going supervision is high, and offers the bereaved children of East Hertfordshire a most valuable service, based on up to date research. (Worden, 1996). The staff group includes nurses, counsellors, doctors, volunteers and teachers.

Meeting the needs of bereaved adolescents in a group setting has been a challenge. Worden (1996) raised serious concerns about their emotional needs. Sleep disturbance, withdrawal and serious lack of concentration have been commonly found in the bereaved young people two years after the death.

Blos (1962), quoted in Riley (1999), describes seven major areas of adolescent development. However, the nature of their socio-economic and cultural circumstances can make achievement of these goals difficult and hazardous for many teenagers, who have been bereaved.

The seven stages are:

1. The adolescent moves from concrete to abstract thinking.
2. Judgment and logical thinking are developed.
3. Social skills, empathy, altruistic and sexualised feelings become stable.
4. Self image has become firm enough to withstand criticism and stress.
5. A sense of individual identity incorporates successfully a variety of internal and external roles.
6. Comfort with a changed body image frees the youth from obsessing about appearance.
7. A sense of self, strong enough to continue to mature with reduced outside assurance.

I will now describe the use of closed groups for bereaved young people meeting in a day hospice setting.

The work has taken place over seven years, the last group ending in May 1999. Each group has lasted for at least six months, meeting weekly, apart from school holidays. The first group was for older adolescents aged sixteen-twenty-one years. The subsequent groups have concentrated on young people in early and middle adolescence. Referrals are taken from the community as well as from the Hospice staff. These groups have been highly valued by the young people as well as parents and referrers. However, they are not suitable for highly impulsive, acting out young people. The capacity to manage some anxiety and the desire to share with their peers is vital. The drop out rate of five percent is extremely low, so I am convinced that groups for bereaved young people can be a very effective way of helping. The experience of similarity and difference is particularly pertinent for young people as they begin to separate from their families and having a strong need to identify with their peers. This issue is a major preoccupation with young people in middle adolescence - i.e. fourteen - sixteen years.

An enormous amount of work needs to be focused on fostering

an early alliance with the young people. (Manor, 1986). In palliative care the group is mentioned particularly early - at the time of death - by the Macmillan nurse involved (Firth and Anderson, 1994). The group leader may see the young person as part of the family work when preparing them for the death of a family member. The group has to fit in with the young person's world, meeting at a time suitable for them, in an acceptable place that reflects their interests. The worker needs to establish a relationship quickly with the adolescent. A natural non-threatening approach, which shows respect and concern, works best (Malchiodi, 1997, quoted in Riley, 1999). Young people referred from outside the hospice do not have the benefit of knowing the building and staff. Their bereavement may have been unexpected and sudden. Therefore ensuring that schools, doctors and youth workers know about the group is essential. Often, the recommendation and endorsement of the group by these practitioners is the reason that a young person joins initially and attends regularly.

Most young people have times when they are preoccupied with living and dying. Ellen Noonan (1983) talks about the stages of adolescence resembling bereavement, in that young people look backwards and forwards at the same time. It is my belief that bereaved people always feel that they are in a time and place they do not want to be. Adolescents share the experience of being different anyway, and bereaved young people may be more drawn to suicidal thoughts as a way of joining the dead person and thus being reunited with the dead object. Indeed these thoughts are present in the minds of many of the young people. Where the group contains members bereaved by deaths through suicide, the leaders have to be particularly sensitive to the needs of the entire group. The importance of the question of assessment and the subsequent make up of the group cannot be over estimated.

Fundamentally, the selection must be based on detailed listening and knowledge of the young person's functioning before the death. A loss history is very helpful.

Dorothy Stock Whitaker (1995) suggests that groupwork is particularly useful for:

- persons who have been functioning adequately, but now face some threat to life or identity;
- persons who have been functioning adequately, but who are in a difficult caring relationship and are experiencing special stress;
- persons experiencing or anticipating some life transition.

The common themes in all these groups for young people are:

- searching to find ways of controlling and expressing anger;
- fear of dying themselves, or of other family members dying;
- sleep disturbance;
- flashbacks about the death and dying and how to manage them;
- lack of concentration;
- feeling misunderstood (more than normal adolescents).

Many children's groups have parents' groups that meet at corresponding times. Because of scarce resources we did not organise simultaneous groups for parents, but provided a place for them to meet if they wished.

In many cases informal parental groups were formed. It was left to the young people to decide whether or not to share what happened in the group with their parents. In general, they probably did. Evaluation has consisted of a simple questionnaire asking about their experience in the group.

Consistently, young people have said that the group helped them. The degree of usefulness varied from a small amount to a considerable extent. Many young people reported that symptoms such as headaches, stomach aches, fighting at school, sleeplessness and loneliness, seen by them as being associated with bereavement, had disappeared.

Young people enter the group within the first few months of being bereaved, although we have had two who have been bereaved in primary school. On the basis of Worden's (1996) research there may be some value in follow- up sessions for up to two years. Generally the groups described have been followed up for six-twelve months after they ended. It is not unusual for young people to keep in casual contact, for example, by sending Christmas cards or ringing up with exam results. Analysis of the make up of the groups showed that there were more girls who attended than boys. The majority of young people were grieving a male member of their family. Is this because their mothers were prime movers in asking for help for them? Most studies show women are more likely to ask for help via counselling services than males. Sibling bereavements were experienced by 25% of the group.

The groups we work with are based on an experiential psycho-dynamic model with the facilitators working with a closed group. The young people are encouraged to work on boundary setting for themselves, with the facilitators taking responsibility for helping to keep to them. The boundaries are about punctuality, behaviour and listening to each other.

My aims for the group are to:

• enhance the member's capacity to talk about difficult emotions rather than act out;
• improve self-esteem;
• help with reality orientation - which may include giving factual information about cancer, dying;
• what happens to dead bodies. Our experience is that children and young people are often excluded from decision and information-giving family meetings;
• help manage strong feelings;
• develop inter-dependence to help with feelings of isolation;
• promote a sense of helping others as well as themselves. The need to help young people feel better about themselves after such a devastating experience is vital.

I shared these with the first group and they added that they wanted to:

• *think about problem solving.*
  The absence of a parent leaves not only an emotional gap and loss of the relationship, but the dead parent's role and function has to be taken on by other family members;
• *explore the nature of their fear.*

Only other young bereaved people can understand how frightened they are and the group is a place to share this fear.

These aims are pursued in many different ways. The use of games, painting and pottery has been important in helping the young people communicate with each other. Games are often regressive e.g. *Twister*. Examples such as these, which are often designed for much younger children, allow the young people the chance to manage feelings around competition. They also like games about food and others that involve having to trust the other group members. Given that the intellectual levels of the group members and their ability to verbalise feelings may vary, the group leaders play an important part in monitoring involvement.

Some groups have wanted some factual information around illness and death. Other groups for bereaved children e.g. Winston's Wish, have used the idea of a 'Doc spot'. In two groups this was particularly helpful and probably reflected the presence of three young people whose parents had died suddenly through illness or accident.

Young people, like small children, are often traumatised by the death. The tendency of adults to protect them from some aspects of death and dying sometimes makes it difficult for young people to understand the process. One young person said, '*When someone dies it's like a glass shattering and you need to pick up every piece of glass with tweezers and examine it*'.

Setting no agenda allows young people to raise whatever topic is important to them. It is not surprising that the groups need to last for several months. The experience of death is recreated using words, drawings and clay. In this way young people can feel understood and make sense of what has happened to them. We know from the work of Worden (1996) that children and young people have a continuing bond with their dead parent, brother, sister or grandparent. The relationship does not end with the death.

Discussion so far has concerned working with cancer patients and their families, but the people who do this work have to be considered as well, and I would like to mention the use of groups to support them.

Working with staff groups

There can be few jobs which are as potentially stressful as working with the dying. If workers are to keep in touch with the pain and distress suffered by the patients and families they see daily, there has to be in-built support systems. Hospices are beginning to employ outside counsellors, psychologists and psychotherapists to assist them in staff support.

In my own experience as a manager, supervisor, worker and group member, group supervision/support can be an extremely effective way of helping groups of staff and volunteers, e.g. through the use of Bereavement Counsellors/visitors. All of us, staff and volunteers, need to acknowledge that we are put in touch with our own feelings about personal loss and mortality on a daily basis.

The use of psychoanalytic concepts is helpful in thinking about institutional processes, particularly the dynamic processes of fragmentation and integration that characterise the inner world of individuals. In hospices staff, patients and families come together in an intense experience, often for quite a short while, and face life/death issues with all the accompanying primitive anxieties.

Is it any wonder that staff stress levels can be very high? Denial, denigration, splitting, projection and idealisation are key concepts, which help us understand what is happening within the staff group. Hospices in the past have suffered from 'chronic niceness' (Speck (1994). Peter Speck makes the point that Winnicott's concept of 'good enough' care helps us to be realistic about what we can do. Staff supervision groups above all else are places where people can think about what has been happening and the impact on them. So often we see the crisis of illness resulting in an attack on the values and functioning of the family, patient and staff. 'People run around like headless chickens'. Staff supervision groups must be task orientated and attendance to overt, covert and unconscious aims will help the leaders to keep focused. 'A moan session' may help to let off strong emotions, but what is learnt? How will the patients benefit? As in all groups the value is in linking, reflecting, confronting evidence and listening to each other. Making discoveries is at the heart of groupwork practice. The staff supervision/support group makes an immensely valuable contribution to staff involved with palliative care. It helps staff feel safe and contained and leads to less acting out. The evidence is in the low levels of sickness and the growing confidence of staff, resulting in a staff group that can confront painful issues and gain valuable personal insights.

I have discussed four types of groups of which I have had direct experience. What is the wider picture? What have researchers found out about groupwork in palliative care?

The wider picture: Messages from research

Bottomley (1997) reviewed two decades of findings regarding group interventions with patients suffering from cancer and confirmed their effectiveness. His paper examines the literature on patients' groups, considers a wide range of approaches and illustrates the mental health benefits reported in these studies. In the field of palliative care the opportunities for using a groupwork approach are numerous.

Piper et al (1992) describes twenty-five loss groups with the inclusion of a controlled clinical trial evaluation of the 'treatment'. They conclude that short-term groups, under twenty sessions, can be successful if they are specifically tailored to the needs of particular types of patients.

Some of our groups have lasted much longer than twenty sessions. Evaluations have been very simple, but nevertheless it is possible to say, particularly with the young people we helped, that they would not have received or accepted any other individually orientated help. Two boys in the group received some individual help but had dropped out.

The categories suggested by Stock Whitaker (1995) and quoted earlier in the paper are entirely congruent with the groups of people we set out to help. The first patient discussion group did contain patients and carers. The use of groupwork to help carers of cancer patients and bereaved adults is common in palliative care settings.

Finally, in order to lead groups, clinicians need to be trained and enjoy being part of a groupwork process. They need to attend to their own supervision and to plan and record these carefully. A group log, kept from week to week, helps in understanding the group process.

Bottomley (1997) stressed the need for groups to be evaluated more systematically. He concluded that methodological problems existed in most of the research he evaluated and suggested that researchers should look at the value of specific interventions for patients at different stages of their disease.

In the first group that I described, most of the patients had advanced cancer and the design of the group was supportive. The second psychoeducational group was for newly diagnosed patients, was much more structured and has yet to be evaluated. All the groups discussed offered help to adults and children who saw themselves primarily as being isolated, different and disempowered. They valued the experience of being with others in similar circumstances and I believe that facilitated groupwork offered them the opportunity to have this experience in a safe environment.

Indicative reading

Hughes, M. (1995) *Bereavement and Support*. Bristol: Taylor & Francis
Piper, W., McCallum, M. and Hassan, F. (1992) *Adaptation to Loss*. London: The Guildford Press
Stock Whitaker, D. (1995) *Using Groups to Help People*. London: Routledge

References

Bottomley, A. (1997) Where are we now? Evaluation of two decades of group intervention with adult carers patients. *Journal of Psychiatry and Mental Health Nursing*, 4, pp.251-265
Brown, R. and Mckenna, H. (1999) Conceptual analysis of loneliness in dying patients. *International Journal of Palliative Nursing*, 5, 2, pp.90-97

Charmez, K. (1980) *The Social Reality of Death*. Reading, Massachusetts: Addison Wesley

Cunningham, A. (1999) Delivering a very brief psychoeducational programme to cancer patients and family members in a large group format. *Pycho-Oncology*, 8, pp.177-182

Doel, M and Sawdon, C. (1999) *The Essential Groupworker*. London and Philadelphia: Jessica Kingsley

Dwivedi, K. (ed) (1993) *Groupwork with Children and Adolescents: A handbook*. London: Jessica Kingsley

Firth, P. and Anderson, P. (1994) Teamwork with families facing bereavement. *European Journal of Palliative Care*, 1,4, pp.156-161

Hughes, M. (1995) *Bereavement and Support: Healing in a group environment*. Bristol: Taylor and Francis

Kraus, F. (1996) Confronting the reality of terminal illness. *European Journal of Palliative Care*, 3, 4, pp.167-170

Manor, O. (1986) The preliminary interview in social groupwork, *Social Work with Groups*, 9,2, pp.21-39

Marris, P. (1968) *Widows and their Families*. London: Routledge

Monroe, B. (1997) *Facilitated Groups for People with Terminal Illness. Proceedings of IV Congress of European Association for Palliative Care, 6-9 December 1995*. Barcelona

National Council for Hospice and Specialist Palliative Care Services (1997a) *Voluntary Euthanasia: The Council's view*. London : National Council for Hospice and Specialist Palliative Care Services

Noonan, E. (1983) *Counselling Young People*. London and New York: Methuen

Parkes, C. M. (1996) *Bereavement: Studies of Grief in Adult Life*. 3rd Edition. London: Tavistock

Piper, W., McCallum, M. and Hassan, F. (1992) *Adaptation to Loss*. New York and London: The Guildford Press

Riley, S. (1999) *Contemporary Art Therapy with Adolescents*. London: Jessica Kingsley

Smith, S. and Pennells, M. (eds). (1995) *Interventions with Bereaved Children*. London: Jessica Kingsley

Speck, P. (1994) *Working with Dying People*. in A. Obholza and V.Z. Roberts (eds) *The Unconscious at Work*. London: Routledge

Spiegal, D., Bloom, J.R. and Yalom, I. (1981) Group support for patients with metastatic breast cancer. *Archives of General Psychiatry*, 38, pp.527-533

Stock Whitaker, D. (1995) *Using Groups to Help People*. London: Routledge

Thompson, S. (1999) *The Group Context*. London: Jessica Kingsley

Trijsburg, R.W., Van Kippenberg, F.C. and Rijma, S.E. (1992) Effects of psychological treatment on cancer patients: a critical review. *Pschosomatic Medicine*, 54, 4, pp.489-517

Windicott, D.W. (1971) *Playing and Reality*. London: Tavistock Publications

Winston's Wish (1995) *A Grief Support Programme for Children. Progress report (1993-1995)*. Gloucester: Winston's Wish

Worden, J.W. (1996) *Children and Grief: When a parent dies*. New York: The Guilford Press

When actions speak louder:
Groupwork in occupational therapy

Linda Finlay

The practice of groupwork in occupational therapy is diverse, spanning elements of both psychotherapy and psycho-education. Although these groups can have different therapeutic aims, they share a focus on activity and require the active involvement of group members. This chapter aims to map the different types of groupwork currently being practised within occupational therapy in Britain. A case study of a group in action shows how an occupational therapy group can evolve over time. A final section briefly evaluates the use of groupwork within the field of occupational therapy.

Introduction

The practice of groupwork in occupational therapy is diverse - perhaps more so than in any other field. Occupational therapists are involved in groups that span a wide range of activities, from psychodrama to woodwork. This diversity of occupational therapy groupwork practice arises, in part, as the therapists typically work in a range of settings - including hospitals, special units and the community - and with a range of patient/client groups who have different psychological and/or physical problems. Thus, a therapist working in an acute mental health setting might run group-based art therapy sessions where members are encouraged to express and explore their feelings. A therapist working in a cardiac rehabilitation unit might offer an anxiety management group. Another working in a medium secure forensic unit might be more involved with teaching skills using a cookery within general life skills group. A therapist working in the community might be offer an on-going psychotherapy-orientated support group.

Although the different approaches advanced by occupational therapists may have different therapeutic aims, they all share a use of 'activity' and a central focus on 'occupational performance' (i.e. how a person functions in their daily work, leisure and domestic/personal activities). It is these features - activity and occupation - which distinguish occupational therapy groupwork from that of other disciplines. In order to give a flavour of what this use of activity to enable occupational performance means, Box 1 gives an example of a practically orientated occupational therapy group.

Box 1. A cookery group to develop skills

Sandra, an occupational therapist, has set up a cookery group for four people who have learning disabilities and who live in a special rehabilitation unit. In six months' time they are due to be resettled together into a group home. The cookery sessions are designed to help them make the move by fostering their sense of independence and teaching them life skills. Through the therapeutic activity of cooking together, Sandra's four clients will, it is hoped:

- learn relevant cooking skills
- develop their social interaction skills
- learn how to share tasks

Description of one session

Having previously agreed to cook burgers, potatoes and baked beans, Sally and Dave have done the shopping. The group session begins as they arrive in the kitchen with their groceries.

Mary rushes to look in the bags and is immediately reprimanded by Sally. When Mary hears Sally and Dave have bought mince, she sulkily declares she does not want any. The therapist, Sandra, intervenes to prevent an argument erupting. Reminding Mary that they had planned the meal the week before, she suggests that if Mary takes part this week she can take part in choosing a new menu for next week. In a happier frame of mind Mary acquiesces.

Sandra now gathers the group around the table to clarify the tasks that need to be done and negotiate who is going to take responsibility for each part. Kevin immediately volunteers his customary role of sorting out the dessert (ice cream and fruit). Dave offers to make mashed potatoes whilst Mary says she wants to heat the beans (the one task she feels comfortable doing). Sandra asked Sally, the more experienced cook, if she would be prepared to allow Mary to help with mixing and shaping the burgers. Sally agrees.

As the group members get on with their jobs, Sandra moves among them teaching relevant techniques and encouraging them to interact and help each other. Suddenly Mary lets out a shout, pushing the mixing bowl containing the mince to the floor. Sandra intervenes to prevent any escalation of this new fight between Sally and Mary, gently asking Mary to express what is upsetting her. It emerges that Sally has undone Mary's burgers and remade them as they had not been "good enough". Sandra encourages Sally to let Mary have another go, but suggest that this time Sally should do more to guide Mary. With much pleasure and a sense of achievement, Mary eventually produces a successful burger. Sally then competently fries up the other burgers whilst showing Mary how to cook her own.

Sandra moves on to help Dave through the stages of making his mashed potatoes. Meanwhile, Kevin is working quietly on his own. As the meal is cooking Sandra encourages the group to work together to set the table - a cooperative task they manage well and in good spirits. Unprompted, Mary places a small flower in a vase in the centre of the table - a gesture which everyone appreciates.

After the meal and the clearing up, the group members reassemble at the table where Sandra encourages them to evaluate the meal and review what has been learned. Everyone has enjoyed the food and they all agree they could probably manage to make the same meal on their own next time. Sally understands she needed to do more to support Mary. Mary, for her part, says that if Sally was her friend she would try to control her "quick angries". The group members then set about planning their next meal.

After the group Sandra evaluates the group. She is pleased with the outcomes seeing that valuable lessons and skills have been learned. She reflects on the way she managed the conflicts within the group and judges her strategy to push Sally and Mary to cooperate was both interesting and successful. Sandra makes a note to be less directive in future sessions to enable the group members to take more responsibility for themselves.

Types of groups

Typologies of groups have traditionally separated psychotherapy from activity orientated groups, implying a separation of task and verbal elements. Within occupational therapy, however, most groups can be seen to combine the two. For this reason, occupational therapists tend to talk in terms of three types of group: those which are predominantly activity-based; those which are support based; and those which are a mixture of the two. (see Figure 1). In general terms, activity groups emphasise the task and end product of the group while support groups value sharing and group process dimensions (Finlay, 1993; 1997).

Activity groups primarily involve task and/or social elements. Task groups aim to develop individuals' skills. They include craft groups, work groups, life skills groups and reality orientation sessions. Social groups (involving dance, exercise, sports and games), by contrast, are for recreation and aim to encourage social interaction. Borg and Bruce (1991) offer their version of a 'therapeutic activity group' which has the explicit goal of enabling change and encouraging satisfying social roles. Here, a range of activities (for instance, games) are utilised to structure patients' participation in terms of making decisions, taking responsibility and gaining social skills.

Support groups focus on communication and/or psychotherapy. Communication groups encourage group members to give each other support and share experiences. Discussion groups, social skills training and creative groups come under this heading.

Figure 1 Continuum of aims and types of group involvement

	Activity Groups		Support Groups	
(focus)	task	social	communication	psychotherapy
(goals)	to develop functional skills	to encourage leisure and interaction	to experience support and sharing	to express and explore feelings
(therapist role)	therapist structures activities and tends to offer support by being directive and occasionally didactic		therapist facilitates group members to participate so is less directive and does more to comment on process	

Psychotherapy groups aim to help individuals gain insight and explore their feelings. This use of the term extends the traditional definition of psychotherapy groups as purely verbal to those which can include activities such as psychodrama or projective art. In this context, Leary (1994) has described a range of psychodynamic and creative activities which aim to promote self awareness, based on such themes as 'Who am I?', 'Caring about each other' or 'My problem is'.

This classification of activity versus support groups should not be interpreted rigidly. Any activity can be designed to fit into the task - social - communication - psychotherapy continuum (see Figure 1). In fact, all the elements may be on offer in any one group but shift according to what the group is doing and according to how group members respond. Members may simultaneously share feelings (psychotherapy) and give each other support (communication), whilst having fun (social) and learning a new hobby (task). Further, it is important to recognise that different individuals may well react differently to the same activity. A role play, for instance, can be experienced as fun by one person, as a practical way of learning a skill by another, and as the trigger for all sorts of emotional reactions in a third (Finlay 1997).

Figure 2 The Next Step Group. Sequence of themes/activities

Session	Activity and focus
1.	Art: 'describing me now and before'
2.	Collage: 'bits I like about myself and bits I don't like'
3.	Buttons: plotting my life story and important events.
4.	Music or poetry: sharing a special piece
5.	Pottery: family sculptures
6.	Psychodrama: family sculpts
7.	Flipchart: Roles and daily activities - planning what needs to change
8.	Role plays and enacting scenes psycho-dramatically as relevant to individuals
9.	"
10.	"
11.	Writing: negotiating, agreeing and writing 'contracts for change'
12.	Painting: 'futures- where I see myself in one year' and an ending group painting.

Case example: 'The next step group'

The following example of groupwork highlights typical concerns, activities and processes within occupational therapy.

The 'Next Step Group' is a support group aimed at helping people who have recently lost important life roles to adjust to and cope with their new situation (Finlay, 1997). The approach is predominantly psychodynamic and treatment methods combine creative or expressive activities with group discussion. The group ideally meets over 12 weekly sessions. A loose structure is offered to the group members (see Figure 2) whereby the first six sessions explore members' situations, concern and needs, while the latter six focus on 'planning and practising for change'. In consultation with the members, the therapists plan each session as the group evolves to ensure that the activities are relevant and meaningful.

In this case study, the 'Next Step Group' works with six individuals with a history of substance misuse who are in various stages of 'recovery'. The process of setting up the group sees the therapists interviewing a number of individuals to assess their suitability and engage them in the idea of group treatment. The six people selected commit themselves to attend all twelve sessions and be active participants.

The initial sessions involve group building exercises and activities designed to help the members get to know each other. To begin with members are anxious about being in the group and experience some discomfort about disclosure and the unfamiliar way of working. In this early stage the therapists work hard to encourage the members to participate, pointing out areas where individual members share certain experiences.

By the fifth session, the members have begun to trust each other sufficiently to express some anger. Open conflict occurs between George (aged 50) and Steve (aged 24) as they appear to project family roles (of 'authoritarian father' and 'deviant son' respectively) on to each other. Mandy (aged 22) joins the fray, attacking George for being overly critical and judgmental. Supporting Steve, she begins to reveal the abuse she suffered as a child from her own father.

In the next session, Mandy is encouraged by the therapists and other group members to enact a particularly traumatic family scene, with George acting as her father. This emotional session proves to be both cathartic and productive. Members work together to help Mandy and George see each others' points of view.

By common consent, at the beginning of the next session the group members agree they are ready to get down to the 'practical business' of looking at their 'next steps' in their new lives. Useful discussion takes place about what precipitates problem behaviours and what kinds of situations might prevent them changing. Over the next three sessions several individuals volunteer to 'take the spotlight'. Martin (aged 39) 'practises' going into a pub with his friends and saying 'no' to a drink. Ellen (aged 26) 'speaks' to her friend who has died from taking some impure drugs - an incident about which Ellen still feels guilty.

The last two sessions are experienced in mixed ways. Some anger is expressed towards the therapists for not allowing the group to continue beyond the contracted 12 weeks. Issues of loss and sadness are also explored, and there is recognition that the group has been an invaluable experience. In the concluding session, where everyone gets involved in a large, messy group painting, fun is mingled with tears. The group members agree to meet for a follow-up session in three months time.

Therapeutic value of groupwork

From the above case examples and references, it can be seen that occupational therapists exploit different learning opportunities within a variety of group situations. This diversity is not surprising when one comes to consider the potentialities of groupwork to a field like occupational therapy. Groups help develop individuals' sense of personal and social identity. Through action and interaction, participants' acquire skills, attitudes and ways of behaving as they respond to the expectations of others and adopt different roles. They are empowered and gain strength as they share with others, both giving and gaining support. In a real sense, as Leary puts it, "In groups people experience life" (Leary, 1994, p.203). The challenge, for the occupational therapist, is to harness these special characteristics of a group, and select active learning and supportive experiences which will benefit patients and clients.

A number of researchers have investigated the value of occupational therapy groups (see: Tallant, 1998, for a comprehensive review). For example, McDermott (1988) considered the impact of three types of group formats (task, activity-based verbal and verbal) on interaction patterns. Task groups were found to generate more positive interactions whilst activity-based verbal and verbal formats enabled greater discussion of feelings. Salo-Chydenius (1996) demonstrated that the verbal and non-verbal communication skills of long-term mentally ill patients improved after they took part in a carefully structured social skills training programme. Trace and Howell (1991) applied Kaplan's (1988) ideas for 'the Directive Group' to working with the elderly. They found the set format of daily games, crafts and exercises improved both task performance and social interaction. Prior (1998a; 1998b) and Rosier, Williams and Ryrie (1998) have researched the value of anxiety management courses which utilise a combination of group discussion, activities and role play to help people boost their skills and gain confidence. In these group contexts, members were observed to lend one another support as they shared experiences and learned new coping strategies together.

Studies such as these suggest that the specific combination of activity and groupwork utilised by occupational therapists offers a unique and powerful tool to teach skills, promote change and encourage social contact.

Turning to research on how clients value their groupwork, many studies (e.g. Polimeni-Walker et al, 1992) have shown that they feel positive about their experiences and that they enjoy the use of activities. Confirming these findings, Lloyd and Maas (1997) fire a warning that clients also need to link enjoyment with understanding therapeutic goals. Finlay (1993) similarly stresses the need for clients to understand the goals of their therapy as part of ensuring their continued commitment, motivation and participation. Other studies pick up this theme returning to Yalom's curative factors. Falk-Kessler et al (1991) showed that both clients and group therapists valued group cohesiveness, hope and interpersonal learning as being the most significant group process factors. In these ways, groupwork continues to be valued, and so utilised, as a specialised but significant therapeutic medium within broader occupational therapy practice.

However, in occupational therapy, as in other areas, the curative potential of groupwork is by no means automatic or inevitable. Group experiences are powerful; they can therefore be destructive just as much as they can be beneficial. Conscious of this double-edged sword, therapists must guide and support their clients while encouraging their active participation in the group experience. The challenge, for the group therapist, is to manage with sensitivity the complex dynamics generated when interdependent people relate to one another. The therapist, too, has much to learn from groupwork.

Recommended reading

Atkinson, K. and Wells, C. (in press) *Creative Therapies: A psychodynamic approach*. Cheltenham: Stanley Thornes
Atkinson and Wells offer an in-depth look at the application of the psychodynamic creative therapy approach. After reviewing the range of psychoanalytical and humanistic theory underpinning occupational therapy groupwork, they explore the practical application of the theory using case examples.

Cole, M.B. (1998) *Group Dynamics in Occupational Therapy: The theoretical basis and practice application of group treatment*. (2nd edition) Thorofare, NJ: Slack
This large textbook offers a comprehensive examination of groupwork arising from different theoretical frames of reference. In addition, numerous group protocols and case examples offer guidance on how to apply the various theoretical approaches in practice.

Finlay, L. (1993) *Groupwork in Occupational Therapy*. Cheltenham: Stanley Thornes
This smaller textbook offers a practical introduction to groupwork in occupational therapy. Part One sets out the basic theory of occupational therapy groupwork and group dynamics. Part Two offers specific guidelines for how to plan, lead and manage groups.

References

Atkinson, K. and Wells, C. (in press) *Creative Therapies: A psychodynamic approach*. Cheltenham, Stanley Thornes
Borg, B. and Bruce, M.A. (1991) *The Group System: The therapeutic activity group in occupational therapy*. New Jersey: Slack
Falk-Kessler, J., Momich, C. and Perel, S. (1991) Therapeutic factors in occupational therapy groups. *American Journal of Occupational Therapy*, 45, pp.59-66
Finlay, L. (1997) Groupwork. in J. Creek (ed) *Occupational Therapy and Mental Health*. Edinburgh: Churchill Livingstone
Finlay, L. (1993) *Groupwork in Occupational Therapy*. Cheltenham, Stanley Thornes

Kaplan, K. (1988) *Directive Group Therapy.* Thorofare, NJ: Slack

Leary, S. (1994) *Activities for Personal Growth: A comprehensive handbook of activities for therapists.* Sydney: McLennan and Petty

Lloyd, C. and Maas, F. (1997) Occupational therapy group work in psychiatric settings. *British Journal of Occupational Therapy,* 60, 5, pp.226-229

McDermott, A. (1988) The effect of three group formats on group interaction patterns. *Occupational Therapy in Mental Health,* 8, 3, pp.69-89

Polimeni-Walker, I., Wilson, K. and Jewens, R. (1992) Reasons for participating in occupational therapy groups: Perceptions of adult psychiatric in-patients and occupational therapists. *Canadian Journal of Occupational Therapy,* 59, pp.240-247

Prior, S. (1998a) Determining the effectiveness of a short-term anxiety management course. *British Journal of Occupational Therapy,* 61, 5, pp.207-213

Prior, S. (1998b) Anxiety management: Results of a follow up study. *British Journal of Occupational Therapy,* 61, 6, pp.284-285

Rosier, C., Williams, H. and Ryrie, I. (1998) Anxiety management groups in a community mental health team, *British Journal of Occupational Therapy,* 61, 6, pp.203-206

Salo-Chydenius, S. (1996) Changing helplessness to coping: an exploratory study of social skills training with individuals with long-term illness, *Occupational Therapy International,* 3, 3, pp.174-189

Tallant, B. (1998) Applying the group process to psychosocial occupational therapy. in F. Stein and S. Cutler (eds.) *Psychosocial Occupational Therapy: A holistic approach.* San Diego, CA: Singular Publishing

Trace, S. and Howell, T. (1991) Occupational therapy in geriatric mental health, *The American Journal of Occupational Therapy,* 45, 9, pp.833-838

Groups
with an interpersonal focus

Punishment and the question of ownership:

Groupwork in the criminal justice system

Liz Dixon

Groupwork has finally emerged as a mainstream and often first choice method of intervention in England and Wales probation practice. In this chapter, important initiatives will be traced and an overview of different models and methods used in the Service will be reviewed. Positive as well as contentious developments that have resulted from the What Works movement and the new accredited programmes, promoted through the 'Pathfinder Project', will be discussed.

The fundamental argument is that ownership - the process of personally validating new experiences, does matter: effective groupwork practice relies on handling spontaneous processes as much as it depends on following prescribed contents.

People who have been found guilty of committing offences are increasingly required to undertake some form of groupwork within the criminal justice system. The main purpose of probation supervision in England and Wales is to reduce offending behaviour and thereby protect the public. The Home Office Minister, Paul Boateng, has instructed the Nationalised Probation Service to see itself as a law enforcement agency. 'It's who we are, it's what we do' (Home Office, 2000, p.1).

Probation Officers are to build closer links with the Criminal Justice agencies and distance themselves from their social work legacy and ethos. Indeed, it took a major campaign to defeat a plan to rename the Service 'The Community Punishment and Rehabilitation Service' (Hignett, 2000). The statutory role of the Service is to 'secure the rehabilitation of the offender, protect the public from harm from the offender or prevent the offender from committing further offences' (Criminal Justice Act 1991, Section 8(1)).

Since the Criminal Justice Act 1991, principles of 'just deserts' have been more explicitly emphasised in sentencing. Offending behaviour is assessed and monitored and supervision is imposed with a view to reducing the risk of re-offending and protecting the public. The victim perspective has a greater prominence in the contents of supervision sessions with offenders. Many of the groups currently being designed in the Service are for people who present as persistent or serious offences ('high tariff offenders') and there is a growing optimism that we can achieve change with greater attention to model, method and script (Chapman and Hough, 1998; Raynor and Vanstone, 1994).

What kind of groups and for whom?

In the past, the development of groupwork practice evolved and developed mainly as a result of practitioner initiatives. By contrast, the present Pathfinder Programme is effectively a top down directive, which is a relatively recent phenomenon. Local Services throughout the country are vying to get *their* group programme validated for accreditation. A brief review of some of the main groups run in the Service at the start of a new millennium in England and Wales may reflect the current mix of models and methods of groupwork in the Probation Service.

Offending behaviour groups

'Offending behaviour groups' have been around since the 1970s. These have been developed for different settings and categories of offenders. One example is a programme called 'Think First' (McGuire, 1996) which involves a combined approach of individual interventions and groupwork. The contents of that programme are detailed and prescriptive and the emphasis is on developing problem solving skills; groupworkers are equipped with manuals and scripts. Other cognitive behavioural groups are delivered in probation centres and officers follow similar guidelines where practice is prescriptive. Within these programmes offenders work on 'exercises' collated in a manual, the purpose of which is to encourage a change in offenders' thinking and cognition.

Ad hoc groups

A variety of groupwork projects have been set up throughout the country where workers are allowed far more freedom. Examples of these are the drink impaired driver's group (Roscoe, 1998), the driving while disqualified groups, anger management groups, and the alcohol and offending groups. These groups do follow a set format, but show considerable variation around the country as officers adapt the programme to their clients' needs. Workers who practice in this way do retain a degree of autonomy and an ability to work with group processes. Some services have formed partnerships with other agencies in the criminal justice system such as alcohol agencies. The aim of the partnership is to utilise the varied and specialised knowledge available and thus raise victim awareness and victim empathy among group members. Sometimes mutual education among workers emerges through such groups.

Sex offender groups

Sex offender groups are mostly run in prisons in view of the nature of the offence and the rigid and entrenched patterns of offending involved (Beech et al., 1998), but there are increasing numbers of community programmes (e.g. Roberts and Baim, 1999). These groups have been innovative and heavily monitored so as to 'measure effectiveness,' and make best use of research and practice wisdom. In these groups, and likewise in domestic violence offenders groups, there is still a high premium placed on groupworkers' ability to hold the emotional tensions surrounding the discussion of sexual and violent offending while facilitating the enabling processes (Cowburn, 1993; Teft, 1999). Moreover, innovative group initiatives continue to develop in the community, as demonstrated in the example that follows, as practitioners struggle to work with damaged and challenging individuals

Sex offenders have traditionally had to admit guilt to qualify for group programmes. Thus, Probation Officers are often left unsupported to do individual casework with sex offenders in denial who continue to present as a risk to the public. However, Roberts and Baim (1999) draw attention to the fact that denial is not as important an indicator of risk as is often thought. Middlesex Probation Service together with Geese Theatre have piloted a community-based programme run exclusively for sex offenders who deny all or most of their offending. Results are positive and officers are relieved to have somewhere to which they can refer such offenders.

Groups in prisons

Groupwork has also become a more established method of intervention in many prisons (Ashe et al., 1993; Fisher at al., 1993). Examples include young offenders' groups, thinking skills groups, groups for those with mental distress, the above mentioned sex offender groups and, more recently, foreign national groups (Chenney, 1992).

The latter groups are testament to the fact that innovative practice depends on practitioners' understanding of group processes and their ability to launch and develop unique solutions. No two prisons are ever alike and foreign national populations differ widely across the prison estate (Hales, 1997; Dixon, 1997). The groups are concerned with imparting information and equipping individuals with relevant knowledge in view of their vulnerable status. The model is very different from the cognitive behavioural methods used in other parts of the Service and reflects more the empowerment models described by Mullender and Ward (1991).

Working with others

The literature on groupwork records examples of working with other agencies (Moore, 1996; Thompson, 1995; Hayden et al., 1999), and the Service has long been convinced of the effectiveness of working across multidisciplinary divides. Hearing information from different sources appears to bring both credibility and vitality to practice. An example of this work would be the drink impaired drivers' group, where specialist agencies contribute their knowledge and skills around alcohol abuse. Road safety officers are also invited to speak about their experiences of the connection between accidents and alcohol consumption. In addition, Probation Officers also collaborate with the creative media. Hayden et al. (1999) have demonstrated how group leaders *can* work creatively within accredited programmes. Drama techniques have been incorporated into these programmes to help reach individuals with different learning styles particularly when offenders struggle with lower level of literacy.

Young people

The previous discussion focused on working with adult offenders. Yet, the criminal justice system also deals with people under the age of seventeen years who are found guilty of committing offences. These young people are predominantly dealt with in the Youth Offending Teams, which takes a somewhat different approach to working with groups.

In the Youth Justice field it is accepted that a multidisciplinary approach to working with young people will best help them desist from offending. The Crime and Disorder Bill 1998 authorised the creation of Youth Offending teams where professionals from education, social services and the probation service collaborate so that young people can receive appropriate guidance to avoid re-offending. Youth Offending teams deal with people who are at a different stage of their life cycle from that of adult offenders. Therefore, workers in the Youth Justice field accept the need to address the developmental needs of these youngsters as well as addressing their offending behaviour. Workers believe that it is their job to help the youngsters deal with life traumas which have left them ill equipped to cope with their own developmental process and so - made them vulnerable to crime.

Work is based on the assumption that most children and young people who offend will mature into responsible, law-abiding adults. The focus of practice is still on preventing the youngsters from re-offending, but the means are less prescriptive. The aim of intervention is also to help young people develop skills and career prospects, and so - address the link between unemployment, poverty and crime.

Groupwork programmes in the Youth Justice service are not totally dictated and prescribed. Instead, the professionals involved design some of the sessions and adapt quite a number of the ready-made programmes as appropriate.

It is true that the *What Works* movement has had a considerable impact on Youth Justice, and cognitive behavioural interventions have been developed throughout the country. However, the Youth Justice workers have not abandoned other useful indicators of effectiveness. Pitts (1999) quotes James Howell's research, a meta-analysis of thousands of youth crime prevention and treatment programmes in North America and Europe. Pitts stresses that

> the analysis points to the reality that successful rehabilitation endeavours tend to be taken by thoughtful people who are offered the freedom to use a variety of methods of intervention in ways which seem sensible in the light of the predicament of the young offender, available resources and new knowledge. Effective rehabilitative ventures are reflexive rather than prescriptive, they respond to situations as these unfold. (Pitts 1999, p.151).

Why groupwork?

Probation officers have long been convinced of the merits of groupwork with offenders (Brown and Caddick, 1993). Groupwork has been seen as an intervention that offers offenders opportunities to reflect on their actions and attitudes, and rehearse new responses and behaviours. The use of peer influence is often cited as a significant aspect of groupwork. Offenders are often more likely to disclose information related to offending behaviours if their life experiences are validated and recognised by others in similar circumstances. Needless to say, in the group they find readily available peers with whom they can so identify. Moreover, challenges from group members themselves have a unique and powerful credibility: those being challenged seem more likely to listen, especially if other group members reinforce the message. Likewise, praise and encouragement from a peer group build up to become a vital energising force that promotes change. The group creates space for movement and change which is not always available in individual interventions.

Bhui (1996) suggests that the therapeutic support of group membership can assist offenders when they are trying to look at the world from a new perspective and effect change. He argues that the current cognitive behavioural interventions '... must surely create a feeling of loss, dislocation and uncertainty, evidenced by the fact that so many offenders find it emotionally difficult to change a lifestyle which they understand and which gives them purpose' (p.128). Groupwork can assist in the process of change by lessening the trauma of exposure and reducing feelings of isolation. Yet, support is not the only purpose of groupwork. This method can also provide a robust forum in which to challenge and confront anti-social attitudes and behaviours with a view to developing alternative responses. Teft (1998) argues that this is particularly relevant when working with perpetrators of domestic violence who often display entrenched behaviours, which they heavily defend and justify.

While Probation Officers have worked with offenders in groups for decades, groupwork has only recently 'come of age' as a method of intervention. A brief history of groupwork may serve to put the current trend in context.

History of groupwork in the criminal justice system

Senior (1991) summarises three historical phases of groupwork in the Probation Service. Prior to the 1970s groupwork was an ad hoc practice initiative used to support vulnerable clients, or clients' families. The purpose was to create mutual support systems among the members. There was little evidence of managerial support for groupwork, and groupwork skills and theory were not an intrinsic part of pre-qualifying courses.

Between 1972 and 1984 we saw the onset of the emphasis on social skills training which led to a proliferation of groupwork initiatives as a useful means of engaging offenders and as a form of active intervention in their lives. New legislative changes at that time heralded the development of the current probation centres. In these centres, intensive probation intervention blossomed and groups became the preferred intervention method. During the 1980s, innovative groupwork initiatives emerged throughout the Service as committed practitioners developed specialised groups for sex offenders and also groupwork initiatives for alcohol-related offending behaviour. The sex offenders' initiative demonstrated the professional commitment to protecting the public and reducing offending behaviour (Cowburn, 1990). That initiative also forced probation officers to consider whether the Service could safely run groups in the open community, because the length of the period allowed for each group was limited and the impact was not yet evaluated (Barker and Morgan, 1993; Sabor, 1993). Cowburn (1990) points out that workers were concerned about evaluation and relied upon attitudinal psychometric questionnaires and limited information from reconviction rates in the absence of more sophisticated research tools at that time.

Evaluation of the effectiveness of groupwork intervention remained inadequate. In addition, it was acknowledged that with some client groups, such as young offenders, one would not always see the effect of probation endeavours until a later stage, which further complicated the evaluation process. Practitioners who worked with young offenders knew that the effect of intervention took time to take root, and so effectiveness could not be evaluated from re-conviction alone (Pitts, 1999). It was recognised that some young people might start to reflect and use their new skills only after a further conviction (Graef, 1993).

Senior (1991) dates the third phase of groupwork history from the late 1980s onwards and summarises the new approach as being characterised by 'offence specific groupwork ... as the new solution to offending and as a core element in a package of assistance and control' (p.287). The emphasis was on greater accountability in view of the changing definitions of probation practice. The focus was on *what worked* in terms of reducing offending behaviour and protecting the public. Evidence of effectiveness had become the all-important criterion in a political climate which demanded value for money and the need to demonstrate reduced offending.

These developments signalled the arrival of the *What Works?* era as officers were made accountable in terms of evidence for the effectiveness of their interventions.

The influence of *What Works*

The *What Works* movement developed to counteract the view that it was not possible to demonstrate effective practice. The 'nothing works' (Martinson, 1974) era of the preceding 1970s had promoted negative expectations and had lowered the morale of the Service. By contrast, the *What Works* era focused on reclaiming practice competency and championed a new attitude to work with offenders.

The Service now boasts a significant body of practice models which have been tried and tested and have proved to be effective in reducing offending behaviour. Groupwork is seen as an effective method of intervention and the prescribed groupwork programmes have been shown to reduce offending behaviour by between 10% and 20% (Lipton, 1998). Cognitive behavioural methods predominate as they scored highly in meta-analyses of what worked. Consequently, groupwork programmes are increasingly prescriptive in their attempt to replicate all the elements and principles of the *What Works* ideology. The literature recommends following a list of principles to ensure consistent practice quality and ensure 'programme integrity'. (Hollin, 1993). These models are expounded in a text issued to all officers, *Evidence Based Practice* (Chapman and Hough, 1998).

However, many probation officers have questioned the legitimacy and wisdom of relying on such a reductionist approach and criticised the wholesale adoption of 'evidence based' practice.

From *What Works* to the Pathfinder Programme

The Pathfinder Programme is a further extension of the What Works trend. This programme comprises specific group formats which meet set policy criteria and which are then accredited for national usage. (Home Office, 1999). Consequently, probation officers will have to restrict themselves to these models in future work. The new accredited programmes demonstrate the confidence the Home Office has in the competency of the Service to deliver specific packages. In this sense, the Pathfinder Programme is a wholehearted endorsement of groupwork as an effective method of intervention. There is now a set curriculum which aims to maximise the potential of a pre-determined outcome, namely a reduction in offending.

Yet, many are sceptical of measures which claim to identify the vast set of variables that influence outcomes. Workers worry that they are being unnecessarily restrained, and that the creativity which has to date been essential to the preservation, evolution and further development of groupwork is under threat.

Moreover, there are few current accredited programmes, and there is some ambivalence about the wisdom of any approach that entails the abandoning of tried and trusted forms of groupwork. To jettison what we know works for what workers believe should work is creating difficulties throughout the country. We do not *know* that groups travel well to other areas as local conditions can significantly affect practice.

Indeed, the adaptability of fully prescribed programmes is emerging as a major issue. When examined more closely the complete reliance on prescribed programmes seems to raise serious concerns, and these all relate to the question of ownership.

Emerging concerns: Questions of ownership

The impact of local conditions on practice leads to the question of ownership. This question was first raised by Henchman and Walton (1997) who described their experience in Avon Probation Service. In that service a well designed and successful groupwork programme ran into problems with the arrival of new staff and the failure of existing staff to engage all team members. Because the team was split, workers rapidly began to experience feelings of isolation and frustration, as they had no say in the programme and were not personally able to make sense of the prescribed package: they had no sense of 'ownership'. 'The presentation of groupwork sessions became staid and routine and there was no shared commitment to development informed by practice' (Henchman and Walton, 1997, p.73).

Therefore, a team redevelopment strategy was needed. The practitioners in that service set about familiarising themselves with the aims, principles and shared values of their practice and then re-developed the groupwork programme with a systematic plan ensuring review and evaluation. That strategy led to a revitalisation of the programme and instilled a renewed sense of ownership among the workers.

Henchman and Walton's is not an isolated example. Harry et al. (1997) summarised Mid-Glamorgan's groupwork initiatives and described how they continued to maintain ownership of their separate programmes by resorting to different evaluation methods and paying attention to the feedback from offenders about what worked for them. The authors showed how they managed to retain their skills and autonomy by preserving a 'culture of curiosity' (Harry et al., 1997, p.116).

Indeed, one criticism of evidence-based practice and the *What Works* ideology stems from its sole emphasis on 'contents': the topics covered during the sessions. The result is often the abandoning of active involvement in the group processes that emerge during these encounters (Henchman and Walton, 1997), as part of developing 'packaged programmes.' (Senior, 1991, p.287). Rigid adherence to models that rely on detailed programmes is justified as securing 'programme integrity' (Hollin, 1992). Within this trend, groupworkers are advised not to allow themselves to be diverted from the programme, but stay 'on track,' even when members raise personal concerns. Rigid and focused attention to programme integrity is perhaps understandable when dealing with sex offenders as such people may manipulate the content of the sessions in order to avoid facing their behaviours. Indeed, current research does show that

Needs related to race

Research into sentencing patterns in the criminal justice system has suggested the existence of institutional racism (Hood, 1992; Moxton, 1988). These studies show that black offenders are more likely to receive prison sentences than their white counterparts. With regard to probation practice, research into the preparation of reports has demonstrated the racial bias in the reports officers submitted to the courts (Whitehouse, 1983; Denney, 1992). There have been many subsequent studies that highlight the inequalities in service delivery and in the criminal justice system throughout the country, and these have led to legislation – namely section 95 of the Criminal Justice Act 1991. This section stipulates the statutory requirement to publish annual race and gender statistics throughout the system.

Brown (1992) suggests that the small group is a social microcosm which replicates the political status and power relations of wider society. Therefore, group leaders need to actively counteract these dynamics by positive interventions and by raising workers' awareness. In response to those concerns, the Probation Service adopted guidelines for anti-discriminatory practice. These guidelines educated officers, informed practice and raised issues regarding the bias in assessment and referral for projects and groups that might serve as an alternative to imprisonment. Nowadays, officers are aware that they have to be ever vigilant and that they have to monitor each other's work to guard against discrimination and provide equality of opportunity in terms of service provisions. Quality control takes the form of gatekeeping of all reports to be presented to courts and prison parole boards.

Indeed, the arrival of self-development groups for black offenders is an example of a 'needs- led' group practitioner initiative . In this instance, addressing the need of black and Asian offenders is deemed vital for effective intervention (Jeffers, 1995; Lawrence et al., 1992). Such considerations are vital as racism affects offenders' self esteem and motivation and the loss of these has implications for their offending behaviour. This is why these groups are designed to inform and empower, to impart knowledge and encourage reflection. (ILPS, 1998). This has been validated by *What Works* and it is envisaged that there will be an accredited programme for black offenders in the future.

Despite this there are still entrenched difficulties in getting officers to consider offenders as prospective group participants and groups are often under subscribed. Some of the reasons for this include poor assessment and lack of knowledge either regarding the groups' 'potential' or the offenders' 'potential.' The poor referral rate to black self-development groups persists. White practitioners fail to identify the needs of their black probationers and are often unaware of what the programmes do and what these offer to clients. (ILPS, 1998)

A question of timing

A concern currently being expressed is the viability of offenders completing programmes if the so-called 'dosage'; that is, the length of time it takes to complete the programme, is too high. We know that for sex offenders and the domestic violence offenders we need extended periods of group supervision. But there is less certainty about the length of time necessary for mainstream programmes, such as the cognitive behavioural/ problem-solving groups, which vary from 8 to 22 weekly sessions. Groupwork practitioners deal with issues of poor motivation, entrenched behaviours and low self-esteem which affect offender's ability to engage and change. For 'medium risk' offenders an eight-week period appears optimal and has been the current model which reflects a realistic period given the changing lifestyles of many offenders. The accredited programmes appear to be imposing the length of each programme without taking such considerations into account.

In groups we have the potential to inform and educate and raise awareness, but as mentioned earlier in this chapter, change will only happen if the individual group members invest in that group. There is a danger that we end up at best merely processing offenders through the system, and at worst, setting up impossible objectives which will increase the instance of breaching offenders; that is, sending them back to the court where a different sentence may be imposed.

Currently, the Service is struggling to uphold its joint aims of rehabilitation and public protection on the one hand, and 'holding' clients only for as long as change can be effected on the other. Maintaining this delicate balance will remain one of our most daunting challenges.

A final note

The group that emerges from groupwork is a dynamic force and needs to reflect the involvement of the facilitators and group members alike. This concern about involvement and ownership accords with anti-discriminatory practice as well as quality control.

Doel and Sawdon (1999) have highlighted the difference between *working in* groups and group*work* and this reflects the potential danger of current trends in probation. In groupwork, the workers bring their skills and creative energies to the group but members' involvement is vital. This is why it is necessary to validate members' spontaneous expressions of personal concern. Moreover, group members respond to workers' observations and reflections on their behaviours and attitudes.

Workers do need guidance about effective structures and skills, but they also need to exercise their professional discretion and have a degree of freedom to innovate and to adapt prescribed structures to meet unexpected needs as well as those officially unrecognised. Workers have to be allowed to own practice too. Unless both workers and group members own the experience as a whole, the overall synergy that leads to the enhanced impact of groupwork may be restricted and the full potential of the encounter restrained. If such processes of owning are overly curtailed workers may fail to use the resources of the individuals in the group and the group's potential is likely to be reduced.

There is a wealth of practice experience among present day practitioners and the focus is now on consistency of delivery as groupwork comes mainstream. The Service has developed considerable expertise in terms of constructive and effective programming and the emphasis on effectiveness and evaluation is a welcomed safety precaution against poor practice. Yet, there is a sense of urgency in the Service about implementing new accredited programmes, which is not matched by a concern for retaining existing skills and expertise that mobilise helpful group processes. This is why practitioners must fight to preserve the wider body of practice theory if they are to meet the new challenge of the future.

Further reading

Brown, A. and Caddick, B. (1993) *Groupwork with Offenders*. London: Whiting and Birch
A book that shows examples of working with processes in groups.

McGuire, J. (1995) *What Works: Reducing re-offending*. Chichester: John Wiley
A good example of fully programmed approaches developed within the *What Works* movement.

Rooney, R.H. (1992) *Strategies for Working with Involuntary Clients*. New York: Columbia University Press.
The discussion about groupwork highlights strategies for increasing offenders' ownership of the group they are offered.

References

Andrews, D.A., Zinger, I., Hope, R.D., Bonta, J., Gendreau, P. and Cullen, F.T. (1990) Does correctional treatment work? A clinically relevant and psychologically informed meta-analysis. *Criminology*, 28, pp.369-404

Ashe et al (1993) Meeting prisoners' needs through groupwork. in A. Brown and B. Caddick (eds) *Groupwork With Offenders.*. London:Whiting and Birch

Barker, M. and Morgan, R. (1993) *Sex Offenders: A Framework for the evaluation of community-based treatment*. London: Home Office

Beech, A., Fisher, D. and Beckett, R. (1998) *Step 3: An evaluation of the Prison Sex Offender Treatment Programme*. London: Home Office

Bhui, H.S. (1996) Cognitive-behavioural methods in probation practice. *Probation Journal* 43, 3, pp.127-131

Brown, A. (1992) *Groupwork..* (3rd Ed) Aldershot: Ashgate Publishing

Brown, A. and Caddick, B. (eds) (1993) *Groupwork with Offenders.* London: Whiting and Birch

Chapman, T. and Hough, M. (1998) *Evidence-Based Practice: A guide to effective practice.* London: HMIP

Chenney, D. (1993) *In the Dark Tunnel.* London: Prison Reform Trust

Cowburn, M. (1990) Work with male sex offenders in groups. *Groupwork* 3, 2, pp.157-171

Cowburn, M. and Wilson, C. et al (1992) *Changing Men: A guide to working with adult male sex offenders.* Nottingham: Nottinghamshire Probation Service

Denney, D. (1992) *Racism and Anti-racism in Probation.* London: Routledge

Dixon, L. (1997) The dynamics of groupwork in a prison community. in T. Mistry and A. Brown *Race and Groupwork.* London: Whiting and Birch

Doel M. and Sawdon. C. (1999) *The Essential Groupworker: Teaching and learning creative groupwork.* London: Jessica Kingsley

Fischer, K. and Watkins, L. (1993) Inside Groupwork. In A. Brown and B. Caddick (eds.) *Groupwork With Offenders.* London: Whiting and Birch

Graef, R. (1993) *Living Dangerously; Young offenders in their own words.* London: Harper Collins

Haines, K. and Drakeford, M. (1998) *Young People and Youth Justice.* London: Macmillan

Hales, L. (1997) Prison groupwork for foreign nationals. in T. Mistry and A. Brown (eds) *Race and Groupwork.* London: Whiting and Birch

Harry, R., Hegarty, P., Lisles, C., Thurston, R. and Vanstone, R. (1997) Research into practice does go: Integrating research within programme development. *Groupwork*, 10, 2, pp.107-125

Hay, A. and Richardson, A. (1998) Women need women. *Probation Journal* 45, 1, pp.36-38

Hayden, A., Hopkinson, J., Sengendo, J. and Von Rabenau E. (1999) 'It ain't what you do it's the way that you do it'. *Groupwork* 11, 1, pp.41-43

Henchman, D. and Walters, S. (1997) Effective groupwork packages and the importance of process. *Groupwork* 10, 1, pp.70-80

Hignett, C. (2000) Punish and rehabilitate—Do they mean us? *Probation Journal*, 47, 1, pp.51-52

Hollin, C. (1995) The meaning and implication of programme integrity. in Home Office (2000) *National Standards for the Supervision of Offenders in the Community*. London: HMSO

Home Office (1999) What Works /Effective Practice Initiative ; The Core Curriculum. (Probation Circular 64/1999). London: Home Office, Probation Unit

Hood, R. (1992) *Race and Sentencing A study in the Crown Court. A Report for the Commission for Racial Equality*. Oxford: Clarendon Press.

Inner London Probation Service (1998). *Effective Practice with Black Offenders*. Conference proceedings. London: ILPS

Jeffers, S. (1995) *Black and Ethnic Minority Offenders Experience of the Probation Service: Summary report*. Bristol: University of Bristol

Lipton, D. (1998) *The CDATE Project - A Meta-analysis*. What Works In Criminal Justice Conference. Manchester

Kay, J., Gast, L. et al (1999) *From Murmur to Murder: A resource pack for probation officers and others*. West Midlands Training Consortium, with Midlands Region, Association of Chief Officers of Probation

Lawrence, D., Pearson, G. and Charles, A. (1992) *Black Offenders Project: Report to the Inner London Probation Service and Islington Safer Cities Project*. London: Goldsmiths College, Dept of Community Studies

Leach, T. (1999) Effective practice: Some possible pitfalls. *Vista* 5, 2, pp.141-149

Lipsey, M. W. (1992) Juvenile delinquency treatment. A meta-analysis inquiry into the viability of effects. in T. Cook et al *Meta-analysis for Explanation: A casebook*. New York: Russell Sage Foundation

Martinson, R. (1974) What works? Questions and answers about prison reform. *The Public Interest*, 10, pp.22-54.

McGuire, J. (1995) *What Works: Reducing reoffending*. Wiley: Chichester

McGuire, J. (1996) *Cognitive Behavioural Approaches: An introductory course on theory and research*. Liverpool: University of Liverpool, Dept of Clinical Psychology

Mistry, T. (1993) Establishing a feminist model of groupwork in the probation service. in A. Brown and B. Caddick (eds.) *Groupwork with Offenders*.. London: Whiting and Birch

Moore, P. (1996) Drama and groupwork: Overcoming the double

whammy. *Groupwork*, 9, 3, pp.320-327

Moxon, D. (1988) *Sentencing Practice In The Crown Court*, 1988 Home Office Research Study No 103, HMSO

Mullender, A. and Ward, D. (1991) *Self-Directed Groupwork*. London: Whiting and Birch

Pitts, J. (1999) *Working With Young Offenders*. Basingstoke: Macmillan

Priestly, P. and McGuire, J. (1978) *Social Skills and Problem Solving*. London: Tavistock

Raynor, P. and Vanstone, M. (1994) *Straight Thinking on Probation: Third interim evaluation report: Reconvictions within 12 months*. Bridgend: Mid- Glamorgan Probation Service

Roberts, B. and Baim, C. (1999) A community-based programme for sex offenders who deny their offending behaviour. *Probation Journal*, 46, 4, pp.225- 233

Roscoe, M. (1998) What works with drink drivers? A short review of the literature. *Probation Journal*, 45, 3, pp.142-147

Sabor, M. (1992) The Sex Offender Treatment Programme in prisons. *Probation Journal*, 39, 1, pp.14-18

Senior, P. (1991) Groupwork in the Probation Service: Care or control in the 1990s. *Groupwork*, 4, 3, pp.284-295

Teft, P. (1999) work with men who are violent to their partners: Time to re- assert a radical pro-feminist analysis, *Probation Journal*, 46, 1, pp.11-18

Thompson, J. (1995) Blagg rehearsing for Change. *Probation Journal*, 42, 4, pp.190-194

Weaver, C. and Benstead. J, (1992) Thinking for a change. *Probation Journal*, 39, 4, pp.197-200

Whitehouse, P. (1983) Race bias and social enquiry reports. *Probation Journal*, 30, 2, June, pp.30-32

No Group is An Island:
Groupwork in a Social Work Agency

Mark Doel and Catherine Sawdon

This chapter explores groupwork in the context of social work in the UK. We describe the range of groups which have taken place in a mainstream social services agency as a result of The Groupwork Project; a training project to inspire and sustain groupwork activity.

We make the case for a systematic approach in which groupwork is an integral part of an overall training programme, available to staff at qualified and pre-qualified levels. We consider the use of a common assessment tool; the signposted portfolio, to assist social work practitioners to gather evidence of their groupwork abilities. We describe a practice model of groupwork which is 'essentialist' and relevant across the whole of social work and social care. What is possible in one social work agency is possible in others, and we draw on the results of a national survey to consider what sustains groups and groupwork.

A note on terminology: We use the term learner to describe the sixty-six practitioners who, at the time of writing, had taken part in the training programmes of The Groupwork Project. The term is not intended to diminish the existing knowledge and experience which these practitioners bring with them.

Groupwork and social work

At a Conference on 'The Social Worker and the Group Approach' arranged by the Association of Social Workers in 1954, Miss N. Dawson, Warden of the Birmingham Settlement, opened the discussion by wondering 'whether British groupwork does consciously try to meet the hunger for fulfilment, or whether it just tries to keep people occupied?', a question with no less relevance now. Since then, authors on both sides of the Atlantic have developed typologies to describe the wide range of groups. For example, Brown (1992: 20-6) describes eight mainstream models of social groupwork. North American typologies have been developed by Papell and Rothman (1966) and Toseland and Rivas (1984), and groupwork is also evidenced in the continental European literature (Heap, 1992).

Despite this sound pedigree, in the UK there are growing concerns that groupwork skills in social work are disappearing, and that even when there is a group it is more likely to be an example of 'individuals working in groups' rather than real groupwork (Ward, 1998). In the US there has been a significant decline in groupwork as a specialism on social work training courses (Birnbaum and Auerbach, 1994). In the UK, there has been a pronounced shift away from collectivized to privatized policies and an increasing reliance on procedural rather than professional practice. Groupwork can readily be cast as yesterday's solution by this 'new managerialism' (Dominelli, 1996).

Speculation about the state of groups and groupwork in social work tends to be anecdotal. For these reasons we have chosen not to attempt a 'satellite' view, but rather to spotlight one social work community, a medium-sized social services department in northern England, about which we do have considerable information. The department is typical of most of the others we would be able to map from the satellite, except for the fact that it is host to a project specifically designed to develop its groupwork services, The Groupwork Project. We cannot, therefore, generalize from this analysis to the state of groupwork in social work as a whole, but we can begin to understand *what is possible*. The experience of The Groupwork Project helps us to map the current scope and limitations for groupwork in mainstream social work.

The groups in the case study

Over the course of the Project, 36 groups have been planned, of which three out of four (27) groups ran, all to a successful conclusion. Table 1 outlines group membership and main purpose (for example, 'to provide stimulation and develop social skills').

Table 1: The focus of the groups

Mixed gender groups for adults [7 groups: 26%* of those run)

#1   Day Centre Users with mental health problems
        to provide stimulation and develop social skills.

#2   Day Centre Users with mental health problems
        to change the focus of an existing loose group, by opening it up to new members and using more structured activities

#3   Day Centre Users with mental health problems
        to develop stress management strategies.

#4   Day Centre Users with mental health problems
        to develop greater understanding of mental health problems

#5   People with enduring mental health problems
        to provide opportunities for social contacts in the community to rehearse social behaviours and gain confidence.

#6   Parents with children are at risk
        to empower, support and inform parents whose children are at risk

#7   New foster carers and adopters managing behaviour problems of under-8s to build on existing skills and learn strategies to manage challenging behaviour.

Female-only groups [7 groups: 26%* of those run)

#8   Girls in contact with social services
        to provide a space for teenage girls to be teenage girls - a 'not-therapy' group

#9   Women with eating disorders
        to provide support and alternative strategies for women experiencing a range of eating disorders

#10 Women with learning difficulties
        to provide support, stimulation and a voice for women with learning difficulties.

#11 Women who have been sexually abused
to provide an accepting and non-directive environment for discussion and mutual support.

#12 Women with severe and enduring mental health problems
to promote self-confidence and greater understanding of mental health issues using a feminist model of groupwork practice.

#13 Women Day Centre Users with mental health problems
to improve social skills and relationships.

#14 Women in the community in touch with Mental Health support services
to promote self-esteem and a greater understanding of anxiety and ways of coping with it.

Groups for children / young people [5 groups: 19%* of those run)

#15 Children who have been bullied at school
to help the children who had been or were being bullied to solve problems, leading to a Working Party about bullying.

#16 Young people in residential care
to improve communication between the young people and residential staff

#17 Teenage boys who have been sexually abused as part of a paedophile ring
to prevent what has happened to them from ever happening again by providing a safe environment for exploration and expression.

#18 Young people who are homeless and seeking accommodation
to prepare the group members for independent living in their own accommodation.

#19 Young people who are homeless and seeking accommodation
to encourage the young people to develop life skills to make a transition from care to independence.

Groups for elders [4 groups: 15%* of those run)

#20 Older people with mental health problems
to provide activities and stimulation for the elders and respite for their carers.

#21 Older people with dementia
to counter social isolation.

#22 Older people with dementia
to provide stimulation and improve the groupworkers' own skills in working with people in these circumstances.

#23 Older people who are confused
to create a smaller group within a larger established group and use reminiscence work for stimulation.

Staff development / training groups [4: 15%* of groups run)

#24 Staff in a Children's Residential unit
to discuss professional issues and encourage team building in order to improve the service with children with learning disabilities and their families.

#25 Senior Residential Social Workers
to provide mutual support and a platform to influence agency policy

#26 Staff in a mental health residential unit
to develop a team approach and coordinate the practices and policies within the unit more effectively, using the 'Quality Circle' approach.

#27 New support workers for people with a learning disability
to train new support workers (working with people with learning disabilities) and assess whether they achieve 'benchmarks' of good practice.

Planned groups which did not run [9: 25% of 36 total planned groups)

Day centre users with mental health problems - an assertiveness group
Support for people experiencing loss and bereavement
Support for parents in a family centre
Helping parents to participate in social services decisions about their children
Weekend drop-in group for people who are socially isolated
Young women who are homeless and seeking accommodation
Girls who have been sexually abused
A building project group for boys in residential care
Staff development group for a new staff team in a family resource centre

Although there was no template, a typical group consisted of six to ten people meeting for an hour and a half to two hours on a weekly basis for about eight to twelve weeks. In general, the groups' aims were focused on individual change or support and were shaped by the learners' perception of the agency's function. This conforms fairly closely to what was described some time ago as the mainstream model in the UK statutory context (Brown, *et al.* 1982).

However, what Table 1 does not show is the diversity in the 'shapes' of the groups, from open-ended to time-limited, closed and open membership, formed and established groups, single sex and mixed gender, loosely and highly structured. The largest and longest-running groups were often associated with settings already familiar with loose groupings, such as day centres.

A common factor for all groups was the voluntary nature of participation and all the groups were initiated by the learners, though there was a diversity of style from 'leader-led' to relatively self-directed groups (Mullender and Ward, 1991). As Table 1 indicates, the main purpose of many of the groups was 'expressive' rather than 'instrumental'; for example, concerned with developing self-esteem rather than aimed at specific, agreed behaviour changes. The move towards instrumental goals is perhaps more characteristic of the probation service (McWilliams, 1990).

Let us take two of the groups as illustrations.

The Boys' Group [#17]

The Boys' Group was for just four 13-14 year old white boys who had been sexually abused, and were survivors of a paedophile ring. The main purpose of the group was 'to prevent what has happened to the boys ever happening to them again'. The group was led by two social workers in a Specialist Child Care Team, a man and a woman. The group provided a safe environment for exploration and expression. It was a closed group (that is, no new members joined), with eight sessions running once a week for an hour and a half. An additional 'omega' session helped the group to say goodbye to itself (Doel and Sawdon, 1999: 263). One of the most dramatic and effective sessions was when the boys drew pictures of what they would like to do to their perpetrator. One of the main themes in the group was trust and the breakdown of their trust in the adult world, and it proved very significant to have a female leader as well as a male. In terms of the portfolio, this co-working was unusual in that one of the pair (the woman) completed a portfolio, whilst the other did not.

The group for women with severe and enduring mental health problems [*14]

This group was called 'The Mirror Image' group by the two co-workers, but re-named the '*Looking Good, Feeling Good*' group by the members [#14]. The group aimed to promote self-confidence and self-esteem, with a greater understanding of anxiety and ways of coping. 'Looking Good, Feeling Good' ran once a week for 9 sessions of two hours. There were eight regular members, all white women, but with a wide age range from 32-60 and a dominant theme was the strong desire to gain access to what was seen as the 'normal' world. Both co-workers were pre-qualified Mental Health Support Workers in a Community Team and both successfully completed portfolios of their groupwork ability, using the 'Looking Good, Feeling Good' group for evidence; indeed, one of the co-leaders followed a computer course specifically to create the portfolio. The portfolios included evaluations from the women themselves, giving testimony to the extraordinary effect the group had had on their lives. Most of the women had longstanding contact with social services, and one of them announced in the final session that the group had given her such confidence that, after many years, she now no longer needed social work help.

The case study

The primary purpose of The Groupwork Project is to improve the services available to the people who use the agency by developing the quantity and quality of the groupwork service. This is based on an explicit assumption that increasing the availability of groups and the calibre of groupwork will expand the over-all range of services and choice for users. This, in turn, will enhance the overall quality of service. The main aims of the Project have been to foster new groups and to support existing ones, and to build lasting networks of information and good practice in groupwork; in effect, to see groupwork become increasingly mainstream in the agency, not merely a 'project'.

Two of the Project's main objectives, then, are to discover what inspires and sustains groupwork in an agency, and what constitutes an effective training programme and strategy. The training programme which underpins the Groupwork Project is part of a menu of post-qualifying courses, though the course is not exclusive to qualified staff. 'Skills in Groupwork'; a foundation item in the menu of training modules, carries 40 credits towards the Post-Qualifying Award (see Doel and Sawdon, 1995, for further details about the training programme). Learners' supervisors are involved in the training programme, a significant component which symbolizes agency support for the learners and an opportunity to consider issues of accountability for the groupwork and the group members (Manor, 1989).

Between 1994-8, the Project trained 66 groupworkers (two-thirds of whom were pre-qualified and a third qualified), with a total of 36 planned groups, 27 (75%) of which ran successfully. These groups reached over 200 of the agency's service users. These figures underestimate the actual spread of groupwork, since further groups were spawned by the Project, though they were outside the immediate spotlight. Moreover, additional agency staff were involved in the groupwork, either directly as the learners' line managers, or indirectly as learners' colleagues with a stake in the groups being run. The Groupwork Project continues, with a sixth cohort of learners planning further 8 groups.

Another element which has helped to promote good practice in groupwork has been the development of portfolios. These provide direct evidence of the development of the learner's groupwork abilities and of the progress of the group. 28 learners have completed portfolios of their groupwork practice (58% of those who have run groups successfully). Although the primary purpose of the portfolio is to assess the learner's groupwork competence, it also provides an important research tool to chart the impact of the training programme and a window on the quality of the agency's groupwork service. Just as important, it is a document which its creator, the learner, has almost always felt proud to own as a mark of their professional development.

An unusual aspect of the groupwork training programme is its relevance to staff working right across the agency, in a wide variety of settings and with people in many different kinds of circumstance. Table 2, overleaf, shows where the groupworkers came from, both in terms of their setting and the client group with whom they worked. Table 3 indicates the learners' professional status.

Table 2: Learners' settings

(n=66)	No. of learners	%
By setting		
Field and Community	37	56
Day and Centre-based[1]	16	24
Residential	11	17
School	2	3
By service area		
Mental Health Services:	24 learners	(36% of total)
Children and Families:	22	(33%)
Elderly:	8	(12%)
Young People:	6	(9%)
Learning Disabilities:	3	(5%)
Adults (general): 3	(5%) (n=66)	

1. *includes outreach staff working from a Centre*

Table 3: Professional status of learners

	No of learners	%
Qualified in social work:	22 learners	(33% of total)
Not qualified in social work[1]	44 learners	(67% of total)

1. *includes a qualified teacher and a volunteer (who had previously been a user of the services).*

The Essentialist model

An explicit aim of the Project has been to develop a model of practice which represents the 'essence' of groupwork. This model must be capable of transfer between settings and service user groups and be relevant to all groups whatever their purpose. The desire for this kind of eclecticism in groupwork is not new (Douglas, 1979, p.viii), but faces an environment which is increasingly specialist and hostile to the generic ideal .

We have described the essentialist model in greater detail elsewhere (Doel and Sawdon, 1999) and will outline here the elements which learner groupworkers in the project found most beneficial to the success of their groups. These essential features have developed out of a combination of the existing literature, the authors' own experience as groupworkers and, primarily, out of the work of the Project itself.

Let us use the metaphor of a house to understand this idea of 'essentialism'. A house has features which define it as a house and without which it is not a house; for example, a roof, walls, doors and windows. In addition to these structures there are conventions which we expect of a house, such as the way the space created by the structure is used to shape rooms. We might also make assumptions about the materials which will be used to furnish and decorate the interior. However, 'house' is culturally specific, so that its overall design and the use made of the space within is very diverse. Some features will be considered essential only in certain conditions, such as insulation in a cold climate.

What, then, are the structures which are essential to groupwork - the 'roof' and 'walls'? The notion of beginnings, middles and endings is essential, in terms of each individual session and also the group as a whole. This is the case even when the group is open-ended. Another essential feature is anticipation, in terms of practical preparations and emotional preparedness, and the specific structures available to facilitate this, such as a personal offer of groupwork to potential individual members (Doel and Sawdon, 1999; Manor, 1988). There are common techniques to make best use of the space within, such as the systematic development and use of action techniques (e.g. coaching or flipcharting) and of interactional techniques (e.g. gatekeeping or summarizing). These 'soft furnishings and decorating materials' of groupwork are as essential to groupwork as the structures, though no single technique is essential on its own and they may be used in infinite combinations.

We need to understand not just how groups work in themselves but how they interact with the wider world. In terms of our house, it is not just a question of the outside structures or the inside space, but understanding the house in relation to its neighbourhood and larger community. The essentialist model is based on a systems framework to help groupworkers work with the group in its broader context. This highlights the meaning which the group has for the various people and institutions with a stake in its success (or otherwise). It also provides a basis for an evaluation of the group's progress; the house might have a roof but does it keep out the rainwater?

One other essential of the model arises directly from the experience of learners struggling to help their groups to move from a collection of individuals to a collectivity with a sense of belonging and purpose (moving from 'I' to 'We'). The notion of *group themes* has proved to be a powerful, integrating force helping the individual members find common cause; often the themes are implicit and require the groupworker's skill to help the group identify them (Doel and Sawdon, 1999: 200-4). For example, Suzy might sit on her anger with consequent physical symptoms whilst Bernie's anger comes out explosively; they have very different responses to anger, but 'managing angry feelings' is a common theme. Note that the group might or might not be called an 'anger management group'; indeed, the name of a group can sometimes inhibit the emergence of other more connective themes. It is mistakenly assumed that 'because this is a group for people who abuse drugs, drug abuse must be the only theme'. Frequently, other themes emerge which are not those which have been named.

The model also has an explicit value base. A central theme in current social work practice is anti-oppressive practice (Dalrymple and Burke, 1995; Thompson, 1993). This incorporates an analysis of power and the oppression of certain socially constructed groups at an individual and institutional level. A parallel development has been the rise of participative approaches which emphasize openness and partnership between professionals and the people who use social work services (Beresford 1993). The experience of being in a group and working as a group has enormous potential to empower the members of the group. Groupwork is well placed to put these ideas of anti-oppression and participation into practice.

The common value base of the essentialist model is a commitment to groupwork which is empowering and that combats oppression. Understanding the sources of power inside and outside the group, including the groupworker's own power, and an ability to recognize and challenge racism, sexism and other forms of oppression are crucial. Returning to our metaphor of a house, one of the crucial questions is who owns it and who has the power to make decisions about how it will be used.

The essentialist nature of the groupwork model has proved relevant to a wide variety of practitioners in diverse settings. The 'essentialism' is inclusive rather than exclusive, and learners are encouraged to make links with other experiences, which do not necessarily incorporate all the essential features of groupwork. (We might call these 'group-like', in the way that an igloo is 'house-like'). However, the essentialist model is not so inclusive that it can embrace groupwork which does not promote anti-oppressive practices.

Evaluating the impact of The Groupwork Project

There is no doubting 'the importance of developing evaluation as an integral part of a professional commitment to social work' (Lishman, 1999: 1). For this reason, evaluation of outcomes and processes has been central to the Project.

The outcomes

Each of the five successive programmes of the Project has aimed to test the effectiveness of the model at a particular stage and to refine it accordingly. There have been outcome evaluations at three stages (see the Appendix for details).

Stage 1

In a discussion of evaluation in groupwork practice, Peake and Otway (1990) point to *attendance* as an obvious measure. We have similarly concluded that attendance of learners in the Project is a good indicator of success. More than nine out of ten learners who started the programme completed it (61 of the 66 learners, which is 92%).

Stage 2

A successful outcome goes beyond attendance and includes the running of a group (to completion, in those cases where it was time-limited). Completion has to be measured relatively long-term; for example, two learners did not complete a group until over a year after their programme finished, yet have continued to run many other groups subsequently and to mentor new learners. Thus far, almost four out of five of the learners who completed the programme ran groups to a successful conclusion (48 of the 61 learners, which is 79%).

Stage 3

One of the Project's aims is to help qualified learners to achieve credits towards the Post-Qualifying Award and pre-qualified learners to gather evidence of their own learning. Completion of a portfolio is, therefore, a significant outcome. So far, almost three out of five of the learners who completed a group also presented a portfolio (that is, 28 of the 48 learners, i.e. 58%). More than nine out of ten of those submitting portfolios achieved a pass (26 of the 28, or 93%).

Given the immense number of factors involved in successfully running a group and gathering evidence about competence at the same time, these outcomes seem encouraging, though the lack of comparative data make this a difficult judgement (Cutmore and Walton, 1997).

Process evaluations

The Project is interested in the quality as well as the quantity of groupwork being practised. The pictures which emerge from the portfolios documenting the groups are very positive, suggesting that the impact of the groups on the lives of services users has been significant. Generally, the groups serve people who are the least powerful (such as women with enduring mental health problems, elders with Alzheimers and children who have been abused) and most in need of mutual support. There is perhaps a paradox that groupwork has helped to put people in touch with their own *individual* strengths and resources.

There has been an impact on the practitioners themselves, in terms of their confidence and skills in groupwork, and in their general professional development. The effect of co-working has been especially beneficial, with 77% of those co-planning and co-working groups being successful, compared to only 33% of those who worked with each group on their own.

Pointers for the future

We have sketched the achievements of the Project, but can we learn from the disappointments; the 8% of learners who did not complete the programme and the 25% of intended groups which are yet to happen? Follow-ups produced no surprises: promotions, pregnancies, work pressures, lack of support in supervision, workload mismanagement, failure to recruit to a group, etc. all played their part in preventing learners from completing various stages of the programme. As we have noted, those who came to the programme as a pair were advantaged, with singleton learners less likely to complete at each stage. Remarkably, no groups which got off the ground failed to fly. Indeed, the evidence suggests that the training model as now refined and the groupwork model as presently developed are both suited to develop a social work agency's groupwork service. These are likely indications that groupwork is viable and achievable throughout much of the work of a mainstream social work agency.

In addition, we conducted a survey of social services and probation agencies throughout the UK to uncover the factors which might or might not contribute to the success of groups (Doel and Sawdon, 2000). What is most striking about the findings from this survey is the extraordinary breadth of factors which are counted as 'very important' or 'of utmost importance' to the success of a group.

A list of 11 factors were named in the questionnaire, all derived from the experience of the Groupwork Project. Respondents were asked to rate these factors in terms of their importance to the success of a group, and they were invited to add any others (in all,

145 other factors were added). From the list of 11 factors, four were rated particularly highly:

- 'Checking the need for a group'
- 'Having sufficient time to plan'
- 'The line manager (supervisor) takes an active interest in the group'
- 'The groupworker's practice is assessed'

It was surprising to find this last factor rated so highly. Indeed, the factors *extrinsic* to the groups themselves figured more than those *intrinsic* to the groups, and this was true also for the aspects which were added by the people responding. In other words, the key factors which enabled or prevented a group were more likely to be seen as contextual rather than as happening in the group. The experience of the Groupwork Project confirms the view that once a group is launched, it is successful and that the serious obstacles to groups and groupwork are related to the context of groupwork rather than specific problems in the groups themselves.

These findings underline the importance of an approach to groupwork which focuses on the organizational context as well as the specifics of individual groups. Whereas the groupwork literature has tended to focus on the internal dynamics of groups, successful groupwork in a mainstream social work agency requires a more strategic approach.

In general, the climate of some practice agencies has been described as 'inhospitable to critical thinking and to the tasks of relating new extensions of knowledge to improvements in practice' (Rushton and Martyn, 1990). The agency hosting the Groupwork Project has undoubtedly been supportive to the development of groupwork, but – like other mainstream agencies – its main priorities continue to be driven by legislation and resources. Individual practitioners in the Project are committed to groupwork, but they are realistic about the difficulty of sustaining the impetus.

Conclusion

Groupwork is a major benefit to a significant number of the people who use social work services. This evidence comes not just from our evaluation of The Groupwork Project in one agency, but also from the pages of journals such as *Groupwork*. The Project suggests that a groupwork service is possible in a mainstream social work agency, and that the essentialist model is one which people who work in a wide variety of social work and social care settings can understand and put into practice. We suspect that the model is also relevant across professions, but this has yet to be tested.

It is difficult to know the extent to which training in the essentialist model is helping practitioners to 'do groupwork', as opposed to 'work in groups'. Interactional groupwork techniques are in evidence from the learners' portfolios and videos, but this evidence also suggests that the distinction between 'real groupwork' and working in groups is not too important. The Project has helped the learners to do both with greater skill and confidence.

Taken together, the findings from the national survey and the Groupwork Project indicate the crucial role which the agency context plays in the success or otherwise of a group. Although the strength of the essentialist practice model has been an important factor in explaining the relative success of the Project, the strategy to influence the *context* has been no less significant.

Individual groups can survive, even thrive, where one or two practitioners show great determination and commitment. However, no group is an island, and a groupwork service requires social workers and their agencies to think and act strategically. Fortunately, the skills of groupwork fit this requirement well.

Further reading

Three major sources for those who want to learn more about British Groupwork in Social Work:

Brown, A. (1992), *Groupwork*. (3rd ed), Aldershot: Arena.

This classic text has grown from a slim book of 100 pages in 1979 to double that size in its third edition in 1992. It continues to offer a very practical and comprehensive guide to groupwork theory and practice. Brown has developed a typology of groups, including details of 'mainstream' models of social groupwork. He takes the reader through Planning, Leadership, Programme and Process, Race and Gender issues in groupwork and Developing Skills and Understanding. A chapter on Groups in Day and Residential Settings rightly challenges an often-held assumption that groupwork is mainly fieldwork.

Doel, M. and Sawdon, C. (1999), *The Essential Groupworker: Teaching and learning creative groupwork*, London: Jessica Kingsley.

This recent text is based on hands-on experience of developing a groupwork service in a UK social services department. The book takes the teaching and learning of groupwork as a theme, with Part One placing groupwork in the context of current social work, post-qualifying training and anti-oppressive practice. Part Two moves from the planning stage of a group through to ending, with practical activities to trigger the reader's understanding and use of a generic or 'essentialist' model of groupwork. The book illustrates a wide variety of action techniques and includes brief examples taken from portfolios of groupwork competence.

Mullender, A. and Ward, D. (1991), *Self-Directed Groupwork: Users take action for empowerment*, London: Whiting and Birch.

Mullender and Ward's self-directed groupwork model is explicitly based on anti-oppressive principles. The authors describe the worker taking stock, the group taking off, preparing for and taking action, the group taking over and, finally, the group taking things forward. The five stages of the self-directed model of groupwork are subdivided into twelve practical steps. The model arises from the authors' research and practice experiences with many groups (some are illustrated in detail in the Appendix), and links are made between social relations in the microcosm of the group and what is aspired to at the level of society.

References

Association of Social Workers (1954) *The Social Worker and the Group Approach.* (Conference Proceedings) Surrey: Fleetwing Press

Beresford, P. (1993) Current issues in user involvement and empowerment. in P. Beresford and T. Harding (eds). *A Challenge to Change: Practical experiences of building user-led services.* London: NISW

Birnbaum, M. L. and Auerbach, C. (1994) Group work in graduate social work education: The price of neglect. *Journal of Social Work Education,* 30, 3, pp.325-335

Brown, A. (1992) *Groupwork.* (3rd ed) Aldershot, Arena

Brown, A. , Caddick, B, , Gardiner, M. and Sleaman, S. (1982) Towards a British model of groupwork. *British Journal of Social Work,* 12, 6, pp.587-605

Cutmore, J. and Walton, R. (1997) An evaluation of the post-qualifying framework. *Social Work Education,* 16, 3, pp 74-96

Dalrymple, J. and Burke, B. (1995) *Anti-Oppressive Practice.* Buckingham: Open University Press

Doel, M. and Sawdon, C. (1995) A strategy for groupwork education and training in a social work agency. *Groupwork,* 8, 2, pp.189-204

Doel, M. and Sawdon, C. (1999) *The Essential Groupworker: Teaching and learning creative groupwork.* London: Jessica Kingsley

Doel, M. and Sawdon, C. (2000) what makes for successful groupwork? A survey of social work agencies in the UK. Paper accepted for publication in *British Journal of Social Work*

Dominelli, L. (1996) Deprofessionalizing social work: Anti-oppressive practice, competencies and postmodernism. *British Journal of Social Work,* 26, pp.153-175

Douglas, T. (1979) *Group Processes in Social Work: A theoretical synthesis.* Chichester: Wiley

Heap, K. (1992) The European groupwork scene. *Groupwork,* 5, 1, pp.9-23

Lishman, J. (1999) Introduction. in Shaw and J. Lishman (eds) *Evaluation and Social Work Practice.* London: Sage

Manor, O. (1988) Preparing the client for social groupwork: An illustrated framework. *Groupwork,* 1, 2, pp.100-114

Manor, O. (1989) Organising accountability for social groupwork: More choices. *Groupwork,* 2, 2, pp.108-122

McWilliams, W. (1990) Probation practice and the management ideal. *Probation Journal*, 37

Mullender, A. and Ward, D. (1991) *Self-Directed Groupwork: Users take action for empowerment.* London: Whiting and Birch

Papell, C. and Rothman, B. (1966) Social groupwork models: Possession and heritage. *Journal of Education for Social Work*, 2, 2, pp.66-77

Peake, A. and Otway, O. (1990) Evaluating success in groupwork: Why not measure the obvious?. *Groupwork*, 3, 2, pp.118-133

Rushton, C. and Martyn, H. (1990) Two post-qualifying courses in social work. *British Journal of Social Work*, 20, pp.105-119

Thompson, N. (1993) *Anti-Discriminatory Practice.* Basingstoke: Macmillan

Ward, D. (1998) Groupwork. in R. Adams, L. Dominelli and M. Payne (eds) *Social Work: Themes, issues and critical debates* . Basingstoke: Macmillan,

Appendix:
Progression rates of the learners in the groupwork project

column	1 (*n*)	2 (%)			
Learners starting programme:	66				
Qualified in social work:	22	33			
Not Qualified in social work:	44	67			

Stage 1: Completion of the training programme

column	3 (*n*)	4 (%)	5 (%)		
Learners completing Stage 1:	61		92		
Qualified	22	36	100		
Not qualified:	39	64	89		

Stage 2: Completion of a group

column	6 (*n*)	7 (%)	8 (%)	9 (%)	
Learners completing Stage 2:	48		73	79	
Qualified	16	33	73	73	
Not qualified:	32	67	73	82	

Stage 3: Completion of a portfolio

column	10 (*n*)	11 (%)	12 (%)	13 (%)	14 (%)
Learners completing Stage 3:	28		42	46	58
Qualified	11	39	50	50	69
Not qualified:	17	61	39	44	53

Column codes:
1: *numbers (e.g. 22 of the total number of 66 Learners were qualified).*
2: *percentage of total number by category (e.g. 33% of Learners were qualified)*
3: *numbers (e.g. 39 of the 61 who completed Stage 1 were not qualified).*
4: *percentage of total number by category (e.g. 36% of the Learners completing Stage 1 were qualified).*
5: *column 3 as a percentage of column 1.*
6: *numbers (e.g. 16 qualified Learners completed Stage 2)*
7: *expressed as percentage of total numbers completing Stage 2 (e.g. 33% of all Learners completing Stage 2 were qualified).*
8: *column 6 expressed as a percentage Column 1*
9: *column 6 expressed as a percentage of Column 3*
10: *numbers (e.g. 17 unqualified Learners completed Stage 3).*
11: *expressed as percentage of total numbers completing Stage 3 (e.g. 39% of all Learners completing Stage 3 were qualified).*
12: *column 10 expressed as a percentage of Column 1.*
13: *column 10 expressed as a percentage of Column 3.*
14: *column 10 expressed as a percentage of Column 6.*

Help as mutual aid:
Groupwork in mental health

Oded Manor

Mental health difficulties are often quite frightening to members of the public and rather demanding for the professionals involved. In groupwork these difficulties are openly shared, and so - may be made more manageable. Groupworkers can help mental health practice by facilitating the experiences unique to groupwork and also by incorporating knowledge developed by others in psychiatry. Three of the aspects involved are particularly helpful, and these will be explained. With these aspects on their minds workers can identify the appropriate groupwork approach more purposefully. Workers can then choose how much to emphasise spontaneous processes and how much to stress pre-planned structured programmes. They can also decide whether the group should be offered within a psychiatric institution or in the open community.

Whatever offer is chosen, all groups are likely to emphasise mutual aid among group members with the intention of enhancing the quality of life of each member. The emphasis on members' quality of life renders groupwork particularly relevant to developments in community care. An overview of the possibilities is offered here.

Feeling weighed down with gnawing pain all round but no physical cause?

Lying in bed at night unable to fall asleep?

Suspecting people of trying to get at you?

Have you ever felt anything like these experiences? You might have done, but the trouble was probably soon over. For some people such troubles persevere regardless of changes in their circumstances. When there is no identifiable physical cause for the suffering we refer to these as 'mental health problems'.

By its very nature, groupwork is particularly relevant to enhancing the quality of life of those who suffer mental health problems. This is so because certain experiences can be facilitated in groupwork far more readily than through individual forms of help. In particular, groupwork is best suited for fostering networks of mutual aid among those who are helped. With the advent of community care, these aspects are likely to be of paramount importance.

Unfortunately, this brief review can merely identify various uses of groupwork in promoting such goals, but sources for further reading are offered.

Who is helped?

Stress, emotional difficulties, and mental illness cannot really be totally separated from one another. In real life these forms of suffering are part of a continuous range, and most people struggle with some of the issues involved at some points in their lives. Many people cope with the upheaval on their own or by sharing the struggle with people close to them. The question is at what point professional help is needed, and what form should professional help take.

Most readers will have heard the terms 'schizophrenia', ' depression', 'eating disorders', or 'anxiety disorders'. These, and others, are psychiatric terms that classify mental health difficulties. Making psychiatric diagnoses is the realm of psychiatrists, and other professionals in the field usually seek psychiatric advice about the conditions involved. Advice is necessary because there is always some risk of diagnostic labels being misused and even abused. When used appropriately psychiatric categories are helpful. These categories help psychiatrists determine the medication that may decrease the intensity of certain symptoms. Such categories can also help psychotherapists who need to appreciate how the person resorts to defences against feelings that person finds too hard to acknowledge.

For groupworkers, the minute details of psychiatric diagnosis are not so important. Yet, there are situations in which it is helpful to know the differences among three major categories: neurosis, psychosis, and personality disorder. I shall offer brief comments about these later, but it is always useful to consult expert textbooks in this matter. Many books in abnormal psychology offer guidance in this respect. A good example is the integrative approach of Barlow and Durand (1995).

For the groupwork practitioner, understanding three additional aspects is probably most important. These suggest that mental health difficulties differ in the following respects:

* The *impact* on the person and others: whether the difficulties are severe or mild.
* The *combination* of the difficulties: the positive and negative symptoms.
* *Manifestation* of positive symptoms: the type of positive symptoms themselves as neurotic, psychotic or that of personality disorder.

Let me suggest how understanding these aspects may be helpful. Due to certain policies, most of the people who receive professional help from statutory agencies in Britain will have been diagnosed as suffering from *severe* and enduring difficulties. This means that these people have come to the attention of professionals because their mental health difficulties have reached such a pitch, over such a prolonged period of time, that they, the people surrounding them, or both - cannot function without professional help. Of course, it is better to address emotional difficulties while these are mild; that is, before they become severe mental health problems. Indeed, many groupworkers focus their efforts in this area.

By the time a person is diagnosed as suffering from a severe mental health difficulty, the clinical symptoms are often only part of the problem. By then the difficulties include a host of other hurdles such as inability to keep a job, inability to make personal friends and sustain such friendship, or pervasive difficulties in being with people in social situations. To acknowledge that some experiences are missing in the person's life, such difficulties are called *'negative'* symptoms. Indeed, these may also be symptoms of prevalent attitudes that other people hold about mental health. Negative symptoms are distinguished from 'positive' ones.

Positive symptoms are behaviours to which the person resorts excessively; that is, more intensely than is the normal range in the person's culture, and also more pervasively; that is, in a wide variety of situations where others in that culture do not resort to these particular behaviours. (Barlow, and Durand, 1995). Positive symptoms themselves are not all of one mould. For practice purposes it is helpful to know the difference between psychotic and neurotic manifestations of symptoms, and identify the manifestation of personality disorders.

In *psychosis* the person may suffer delusions and hallucinations as is typical in schizophrenia. The delusions are often that the person is someone else; for example Mother Theresa or Jesus. Hallucinations often involve the person in imagining events that do not take place; for example, that someone urges her or him to do something through the television or even through the walls.

In *neurosis* such delusions and hallucinations are not typical. Instead, acute emotional suffering is involved; such as depression, and various physical disturbances may appear; such as profuse sweating and heart palpitations that accompany anxiety.

In certain types of *personality disorders* the person shows long term pervasive and enduring tendencies to be involved in stressful relationships without expressing the distress associated with neurotic difficulties nor showing the signs of psychotic symptoms (see Barlow and Durand, 1995. pp.515-551 for details). In recent decades professional help with personality disorder has become rather specialised. In Britain, the Henderson Hospital in Surrey leads this specialisation. Their emphasis on working with groups could be learnt by many others, but will not be discussed here.

In general, the distinction between positive and negative symptoms can easily lead to a chicken and egg question: which one causes the other. Yet, on the basis of current knowledge this is not really a fruitful question. It is not very sound to decide in advance that only one type of symptoms: either positive or negative, should always be the focus of help. Far more helpful is to appreciate that negative symptoms: the interpersonal and social disabilities, can exacerbate positive symptoms and even lead to relapse after the positive symptoms subside. Equally, positive symptoms can give rise to various forms of negative ones. This impact of positive symptoms may be due to the sufferer losing confidence in interpersonal and social situations. That impact may be due also to the ways other people react to someone who is struggling with mental health difficulties. The reality is that one type of symptoms continuously leads to the other, and so professional help is needed for both.

Here is how understanding these differences may influence working with groups.

Groupwork in mental health

Small groups have been used in mental health from the middle of the Second World War. Current approaches have emerged out of decades of practice and these will be identified here.

By now, Cognitive-Behavioural group counselling addresses mainly the positive symptoms (Scott and Stradling, 1998). Group psychotherapy tends to focus on members' internal worlds; the intra-personal processes, that give rise to positive symptoms (for an example, see Schermer and Pines, 1999). The work of Yalom (1995) has been pivotal in this sphere.

In *groupwork* the emphasis is usually on the negative symptoms. Groupwork addresses people's interpersonal and social situations. Interpersonal and social issues include a wide range of concerns: continuous emotional support, education and finding work, leisure pursuits, financial matters, legal protection, family relationships, socialising, and health. At times, it is also necessary to respond to unintended consequences of psychiatric treatments; for example, the loss of power, or the lack of information that helps making sense of treatment (Read and Reynolds, 1996).

So, within groupwork practice emotional needs are as important as practical ones, and dealing with the external social world is as vital as developing the relationships among the members of each group. The term 'quality of life' has been adopted to refer to all these concerns (Oliver et al. 1996). *The main focus of groupwork is the quality of life of people suffering from mental health problems.*

What happens in the group

Joy, fear, curiosity, despair, hopes, faith - all, and many more, are common experiences of groupwork in mental health. Because of the emphasis on members' quality of life, these groups often address the totality of each member's situation. This all-embracing nature of groupwork often turns the group into an intensely important focus for their members.

Major helpful aspects of groups have been mapped out by Yalom (1995, 69-105), who called them 'curative factors'. Yalom's research was conducted in group psychotherapy. This is why not all of his thirteen curative factors are always emphasised in groupwork. Of those thirteen, seven stand out as particularly relevant to groupwork. The seven helpful aspects are the following:

Altruism

Gaining self-respect by helping someone else. Increased self-respect can energise people to pursue other changes in their lives.

Group cohesion

Belonging to a group of people who understand and accept the person. Enhanced sense of belonging can encourage people to co-ordinate their efforts with others.

Universality

Realising that other people suffer from difficulties that are similar to one's own: the experience of being 'in the same boat'. This form of validation tends to decrease the person's anxiety about being 'odd', and even an 'outcast'. Instead, the person tends to accept the difficulties and concentrate on what she or he can do about the situation.

Interpersonal learning

Observing and rehearsing new skills of coping with stressful situations. Within the supportive climate of the group each member can safely consider changes in their behaviour. Exactly because the group situation is artificial, mistakes can be readily put right and these have no consequences outside the group. Therefore, each member is free to experiment with new behaviours inside the group and only then apply the changes in real life. Then each member reports back to the group how she or he attempted these changes between sessions. The feedback received by each member should be constructive and supportive and so - should serve to reinforce the member's motivation and confidence in trying to change further. In this sense the group is a true rehearsal stage for coping with the world outside.

Guidance

Receiving direct suggestions about what to do in difficult and new situations. Simply enlarging the range of possible actions open to each member seems to encourage further attempts to change.

Identification

Finding someone in the group the person appreciates to the point of adopting him or her as a model. Provided the person chosen is an enabling model, the new solutions are associated with respect and affection through such identification, and so - may be tried more enthusiastically. When such a role model is another group member, rather than a worker, the impact on the person is often even stronger.

Instillation of hope

Deriving encouragement from seeing others getting better. At times, action does speak louder than words. Direct evidence that improvement is possible can encourage members to try changes more than any verbal reassurance given to them.

Perhaps it is this range of powerful experiences that explains why members often form rather intense attachment to their group. Workers do not always realise how central the group is for the members, and it seems important that they are aware of such underlying feelings. Because of their roles, workers are often made the symbols of this intense attachment - the more unstructured the group, the more so. This symbolic function is particularly important when members find it difficult to express their intimate feelings. I still remember preparing a group in a day centre for my leaving as I was offered another job. In spite of weeks of sharing my concern about leaving, the day after I left one member was so upset that he began throwing chairs around the room. That member did suffer from psychotic difficulties but had never resorted to physical aggression before.

Mental health groups can touch the depth of human longing, and so - workers and clients must have the appropriately supportive environment in which to contain the eruptions involved.

Usually a small number of members are involved in each group: between eight to twelve members, and these groups are often led by two workers. A great deal depends on members' needs and the setting in which the group is offered. In some mental health clubs group processes evolve through informal activities. In such clubs the emphasis is on enabling members to just be with one another comfortably and chat together informally. At the other end of the range, specific campaigns are planned through highly structured groups to improve members' social conditions.

In between, is a large array of experiences: exploring the ups and downs of daily living, expressing feelings through art and music, planning and organising leisure pursuits, clarifying financial rights, dealing with landlords, planning further education, or rehearsing job interviews.

Whatever the contents, the emphasis of groupwork is usually on fostering the ability of members to help one another rather than increase their need to depend on the workers. Members are actively encouraged to listen to each other *during* the sessions and express their feelings, opinions and advice as they go along. Members are also encouraged to support one another *between* sessions. Support may be emotional: when members telephone one another at times of stress. Support may also be practical; for example, accompanying someone to a job interview.

The aim is very much to extend the group experience into daily life so that a supportive network begins to operate among the members in between group sessions and certainly when the group comes to its end. In this sense groupwork goes beyond the seven curative factors mentioned earlier. Groupwork adds to these the help that members extend to one another outside the group. This added aspect is usually called 'mutual aid' (Shulman, 1999).

What we know from research

Roth and Fonagy (1996, p.10) comment that group psychotherapy combines many different orientations, which makes it relatively difficult to research. This is certainly true for groupwork. While such an eclectic stance is helpful, the outcomes are not easily researched.

A starting point can be to map out the various possibilities. This is what Bond and De Graaf-Kaser (1990) did by creating the typology used to guide the present discussion. Bond and De Graaf-Kaser suggested that groups varied along two major aspects: *the methods* employed by the workers, and *the settings* in which these groups are offered.

Here are some examples of these groups. These have been classified according to a modified version of the framework proposed by Bond and De Graaf-Kaser (1990):

Now these aspects will be discussed in some detail.

Methods

The methods of groupwork depend on group members' needs. Like all helping relationships, groupwork methods are various combinations of process and structure and also world views (Sluzki, 1983).

Process

'What do you feel now?' 'How is John's silence affecting you?' Such questions elicit members' involvement in the immediate experience of their group. The more the workers enable spontaneous exchanges among members, particularly when these revolve around members' immediate experiences in the group, the more *processes* are emphasised. Major examples of process

	Methods	
	Emphasising process	*Emphasising structure*
Setting		
Psychiatric	Group psychotherapy	Skills training
	Support groups	Educational groups
	Therapeutic community	
Open Community	Support groups	
	Psychosocial rehabilitation	Skills training
	Self-help groups	Educational groups
	Drop-in centres	Therapeutic community
	Club house	Users' involvement groups

oriented practice can be found in client-centred groups that draw their inspiration from the work of Carl Rogers (1970).

However, the range of process oriented groups has grown immensely. Only a few examples can be offered here. Examples of applications that emphasise processes are:

- Ball and Norman's (1996) use of art therapy within a psychodynamic framework for helping women with eating disorders,
- Fitzsimons and Levy's (1996-7) use of such materials for working with young people who suffer similar difficulties,
- Cwikel and Oron's (1991) use of free discussion and role play with people who suffer long term difficulties associated with schizophrenia, or
- Trevithick's (1995) psychodynamic-feminist approach to helping depressed women.

Before process oriented groups are offered it is well to remember that spontaneous expression of very personal experiences can be too confusing and even too frightening for some people. It is better to assess in advance the extent that people who are invited to such groups are likely to benefit from such exposure.

On the whole, groups that enable spontaneous expression of very personal experiences seem more helpful for those who have not suffered delusions and hallucinations involved in psychosis; that is, for people who struggle with neurotic symptoms such as anxiety and depression.

Structure

'Today we shall talk about being black' or: 'Let's go round and say one good thing that happened to each of us since we met last week' - these are two examples of structured interventions. The more pre-planned and programmed the sessions the more structured interventions are emphasised. Many psycho-educational groups are of this type. Based on a cognitive -behavioural theory, these have been very fully described and explained by Brown (1998).

In most psycho-educational groups members are not deliberately encouraged to express intense personal feelings spontaneously. Therefore, this approach seems suitable for people who are not likely to benefit from very spontaneous disclosures. Structured approaches are important in helping with long-term enduring problems. Many people who struggle with psychotic symptoms prefer such structured approaches, but others seem to benefit too.

Examples of applying structured approaches include:

- Randall and Walker's (1988) task-centred problem solving approach to helping people who suffer from schizophrenia,
- Birrell Weisen's (1991) use of structured discussion followed by physiological exercises to help people with stress and anxiety,
- Thomas and Coleman's (1997-8) use of games, outings, and even gardening to enhance sensory orientation with frail older adults, and
- Gallant et al.'s (1997-8) way of facilitating verbal responses to folk songs in a couples group where alcohol abuse is a problem.

Structured approaches are used even more widely during community meetings in day and residential settings. These approaches are also prevalent in day centres that follow the Club

House model, where activities that help members to find employment are emphasised. In drop-in clubs, where socialising informally is the major goal, structured approaches are very common, as is the case in various user involvement groups. Many of these uses of groups are described in the comprehensive book by Oliver et al. (1996).

The setting

The setting for groupwork may be of two major types: psychiatric institutions or the open community.

Some groups are offered in a *psychiatric institution*; such as a hospital, or a day hospital. These settings are usually led and co-ordinated by a psychiatrist, but others; notably, psychologists, nurses, occupational therapists, and social workers, often actually work with the groups. Psychiatric settings provide the safety required in case group members unexpectedly need medical interventions such as an increased dosage of medication. Therefore, these groups may be particularly suitable for people who suffer from severe mental health difficulties. However, safe as they are - psychiatric settings also surround members with the medical aids and signs that can perpetuate disabling stigmas (Prior, 1993).

Various versions of the therapeutic community model (Campling and Haigh, 1999) fall within this category. Of the examples already mentioned, the work of Cwikel and Oron (1991) with people who suffer long terms effects of schizophrenia, and that of Randall and Walker (1988) with a similar population, illustrate groupwork practice very well.

Other groups are offered in the *open community* where most group members live. These groups may be held in their own or specially rented accommodation, or in a church hall, in a local school, or in a youth centre. The workers may not be accountable to psychiatrists although they always liaise and consult with them. The workers' professional background may vary considerably: social workers, nurses, occupational therapists, art therapists, and teachers of adult education may all work together with such groups. The work of MIND and the Richmond

Fellowship in Britain, various mental health hostels and mental health day centres - managed by social services departments (Bano, 1989; Petch, 1992), and many self-help groups (Wilson, 1995), are prime example of such settings. The more recent introduction of local community mental health teams may expand this variety further.

Because of their openness to the environment such groups may be more suitable for people whose needs are mainly to do with negative symptoms of relatively lower severity and these may include symptoms of psychotic as well as neurotic nature.

Specific examples of practice in these situations can be found in the work of Ball and Norman (1996), Birrell Weisman (1991) Gallant et al. (1997-8), Fitzsimons and Levy (1996-7), Hughes Schneewind (1996), Thomas and Coleman (1997-8), as well as Trevithick (1995). Of course, other groups are offered in the open community too; among them the day centres run along the Club House model (Oliver et al. 1996, pp.209-222), and users involvement groups (Wilson, 1996).

Practice in community settings lacks the safety provided by the medical profession in psychiatric institutions and, therefore, it may not be suitable for everybody. Yet, groups in the open community are often offered within a rather more informal culture than those conducted within psychiatric settings. This is why community groups are sometimes seen as more accessible to clients than groups in psychiatric settings - particularly by people who worry about the stigma attached to receiving psychiatric help.

World views

Of course, world views matter, although the framework suggested by Bond and De Graaf-Kaser (1990) does not include them. Some groups emphasise containment and people's ability to be with one another as a primary value; drop-in clubs are a good example. Other groups stress the importance of gaining added control over resources such as accessible leisure facilities. These are often groups that focus on empowerment (Mullender and Ward, 1991). A third strand may well be the groups who further emphasise the quality of relationships among group members; including their personal relationships outside the group (Butler and Wintram, 1991). It is also possible to let go of any fixed idea of how we should all be. Instead, members may be encouraged to continuously discover how to be themselves in relation to others - who are bound to be different. This orientation is the hallmark of the Human Potential movement. Originating from the work of Maslow (1968), this movement has had considerable influence on mental health practice. A growing concern of all mental health groups is the handling of power related to differences of gender, race, sexuality, and religion (Abel et al., 1996; Kareen and Littlewood, 1992; Fernando, 1995).

Indeed, all these values may or may not be combined, but each influences the experiences in the group.

Current context of practice

No group is an island: social policy decisions and the organisational structures that stem from these decisions influence each and every group. The current context of offering groupwork in mental health is bound to be influenced by the emphasis on community care (Brooker and Repper, 1998), and its implementation through the Care Programme Approach (Forester, 1997; Shepherd et al, 1995), particularly when groups are offered in the open community. Behind the Care Programme Approach is the intention to closely co-ordinate various means of meeting the different needs of people who suffer from mental health difficulties; mainly severe and enduring ones.

Within this approach one worker co-ordinates the involvement of all others. This key worker may come from various disciplines: social work, nursing, occupational therapy, or psychology. The co-ordinator oversees the provisions of many different services. Here is a typical list:

- continuous psychiatric assessment and medication,
- risk assessment and prevention,
- therapeutic interventions,

- accommodation,
- employment,
- legal and financial matters leisure,
- socialising,
- family relationships,
- the various forms of discrimination faced by the people concerned.

The Care Programme Approach depends on identifying achievable goals for each client at each point in time, pursuing these goals systematically, and revising these goals as and when appropriate. When achievable goals are emphasised closer monitoring of the impact of the group on each of its members is necessary. This requirement for close monitoring should not be a problem for groupworkers as good groupwork practice has always stressed the need for detailed observation. However, groupworkers may have to learn more about communicating their observations to other professionals who are not involved in the work itself.

Clearly, the thrust of the Care Programme Approach is multi-disciplinary: nurses (Brooker, 1990), occupational therapists (Finlay, 1997), and social workers (Ulas and Connor, 1999) are expected to work far more closely together. There is no reason why groupwork should not thrive within this diversity.

Pointers for the future

The future of groupwork in mental health is not entirely clear. Here I can only raise three main issues.

Wider acceptance

As yet, the practice of the Care Programme Approach has not shown clear signs of drawing on the strengths of groupwork systematically. Indeed, one of the issues that has to be raised now is the relevance of groupwork to community care.

Most of the practice of community care comprises individual forms of help. Valuable as these are, individual relationships are not likely to facilitate the curative factors of groupwork identified by Yalom (1995). By their nature, individual counselling and individual casework are offered in private: these methods do not directly and simultaneously involve the peers of each client. In groupwork other group members are potential peers for each client, and they are already present - in the same room. This is why groupwork offers more possibilities to promote altruism, universality, interpersonal learning, and the instillation of hope. This is also why mutual aid is far more likely to arise through groupwork than in any form of individual help.

Incorporating the Care Programme Approach

Policy makers will have to be convinced of these arguments, but practitioners themselves can help a great deal too. Sharing aspects of psychiatric knowledge mentioned before is necessary but it is not sufficient. Most groupworkers in the open community depend on receiving referrals from other professionals. Therefore, it is vital that these workers are familiar with the Care Programme Approach and are able to co-ordinate their efforts within this framework.

Training, organisational support, and supervision

Impressions from the field are that many workers, from different disciplines, do practice groupwork in mental health, but how they practice is far less clear. Accounts suggest that some workers are highly trained and closely supervised while others make up their own approach to groupwork without being supported or guided. The latter seem to begin from the beginning - forfeiting the accumulated knowledge of many previous generations of mental health group workers. Indeed, while group psychotherapists are backed up by very rigorous training and supervision, many groupworkers seem to be left on their own - exploring practice through trial and error rather than drawing on relevant existing knowledge.

Facilitating the seven helpful aspects of groupwork mentioned before and fostering of mutual aid, are not automatically guaranteed. These facilitative conditions are not likely to arise just because the workers believe in their value and intend the group to be helpful. Although some workers seem to possess a natural flair for groupwork, most need to learn how to facilitate conditions that give rise to the helpful aspects of groupwork. Still, even training itself is not enough. Training helps a great deal, but very few trainers would be comfortable simply prescribing behaviours that each groupworker should display. Techniques and methods can and should be taught, yet personal judgement will always be needed. So, workers do have to be trained and their personal judgement developed while they are continuously supported and supervised.

To summarise: the practice of community care can draw on groupwork more widely, and groupworkers can incorporate aspects of the Care Programme Approach into their practice. At the same time, there seems to be a need for consistent and coherent training in groupwork for mental health. Such training will have to be sustained through organisational support and professional supervision. Of course all these efforts will have to be linked to further research. A unifying theory embracing all the diverse versions of groupwork may then emerge.

Acknowledgements

I would like to thank Charlotte Heath, Harold Marchant, Lesley Oppenheim, and Bernard Ratigan for their editorial comments on various versions of this text.

Introductory reading

Bond, G. and De Graaf-Kaser, R. (1990) Group approaches for persons with severe mental illness: A typology. *Social Work with Groups*, 13, 1, pp.21-36
A sound framework for classifying mental health groups.

Kaplan, K.L. (1988) *Directive Group Therapy: Innovative mental health treatment.* Thorofare, NJ: Slack Inc
An articulate approach to working in structured ways without losing sight of the processes involved.

MacKenzie, K.R. (1997) *Time-Managed Group Psychotherapy*. London: American Psychiatric Press
A range of group approaches chosen according to the psychiatric condition of the client. The particular value of this approach is in combining structured approaches while also facilitating the processes involved in group dynamics.

Oliver, J., Huxley, P. Bridges, K. and Mohamad, H. (1996) *Quality of Life and Mental Health Services*. London: Routledge
An overview of research into the quality of life of people who suffer from mental health difficulties.

Wilson, J. (1995) *How to Work with Self-Help Groups*. Aldershot: Ashgate
A very practical guide to facilitating users' involvement.

References

Abel, K., Buszweig, M., Davison, S., Johnson, S. and Staples, E. (eds.) (1996) *Planning Community Mental Health Services for Women*. London: Routledge

Ball, J. and Norman, A. (1996) 'Without the group I'd still be eating half the Co-op: An example of groupwork with women who use food. *Groupwork*, 9, 1, pp.48-61

Bano, B. (1989) *Development of the Social Climate In a Mental Health Centre*. in A. Brown and R. Clough (eds.) *Groups and Groupings: Life and work in day and residential centres*. London: Tavistock/Routledge

Barlow, D.H. and Durand, V.M. (1995) *Abnormal Psychology: An integrative approach*. London: Brooks/Cole

Birrell Weisen, R. (1991) Evaluative study of groupwork for stress and anxiety. *Groupwork* 4, 2, pp.152-162

Bond, G. and De Graaf-Kaser, R. (1990) Group approaches for persons with severe mental illness: a typology. *Social Work with Groups*, 13, 1, pp.21-36

Brooker, C. and Repper, J. (eds.) (1998) *Serious Mental Health Problems in the Community: Policy, practice and research*. London: Balliere Tindall

Brooker, C. (1990) *Community Psychiatric Nursing*. London: Chapman & Hall

Brown, N.W. (1998) *Psycho-Educational Groups.* Bristol: Taylor and Francis

Butler, S. and Wintram, C. (1991) *Feminist Groupwork.* London: Sage

Campling, P. and Haigh, R. (eds.) (1999) *Therapeutic Communities: Past, present and future.* London: Jessica Kingsley

Cwikel, J. and Oron, A. (1991) A long-term group for chronic schizophrenic outpatients: A quantitative and qualitative evaluation. *Groupwork,* 4, 2, pp.163-177

Gallant, W.A., Gallant, M.D., Gorey, K.M. Holosko, M.J., and Siegel, S. (1997-8) The use of music in group work with out-patient alcoholic couples: A pilot investigation. *Groupwork,* 10, 2, pp.155-174

Fernando, S. (ed) (1995) *Mental Health in a Multi-Ethnic Society.* London: Routledge

Finlay, L (1997) Groupwork. in: J. Creek (ed.) *Occupational Therapy and Mental Health.* New York: Churchill Livingston

Fitzsimons, J. and Levy, R. (1996-7) An art therapy group for young people with eating disorders. *Groupwork,* 9, 3, pp.283-291

Forester, S. (ed.) (1997) *The A-Z of Community Mental Health Practice.* Cheltenham: Stanley Thorns

Hughes Schneewind, E. (1996) Support groups for families of confused elders: Issues surrounding open peer-led groups. *Groupwork,* 9, 3, pp.303-319

Kaplan, K.L. (1988) *Directive Group Therapy: Innovative mental health treatment.* Thorofare, NJ: Slack Inc

Kareen, J and Littlewood, R. (eds.) (1992) *Intercultural Therapy: Themes, interpretations and practice.* Oxford: Blackwell

MacKenzie, K.R. (1997) *Time-Managed Group Psychotherapy.* London: American Psychiatric Press

Maslow, A.H. (1968) *Towards a Psychology of Being.* (2nd ed) New York: D. van Nostrand,

Mullender, A. and Ward, D. (1991) *Self-Directed Groupwork: Users take action for empowerment.* London: Whiting and Birch

Oliver, J., Huxley, P. Bridges, K. and Mohamad, H. (1996) *Quality of Life and Mental Health Services.* London: Routledge

Petch, A. (1992) *At Home in the Community: An evaluation of supported accommodation for people with mental health problems.* Aldershot: Ashgate

Prior, L. (1993) *The Social Organization of Mental Illness.* London: Sage

Randall, L. and Walker, W. (1988) Supporting voices: Groupwork with people suffering from schizophrenia. *Groupwork*, 1, 1, pp.60-66

Read, J. and Reynolds, J. (1996) *Speaking our Minds: An anthology*. London: MacMillan Press

Rogers, C. (1970) *Encounter Groups*. New York: Harper and Row

Roth, A. and Fonagy, P. (1996) *What Works for whom? A critical review of psychotherapy research*. London: The Guilford Press

Schermer, V.L. and Pines, M. (eds.) (1999) *Group Psychotherapy of the Psychoses*. London: Jessica Kingsley

Scott, M.J. and Stradling, S.G. (1998) *Brief Group Counselling: Integrating individual and group cognitive-behavioural approaches*. Chichester: John Wiley

Sluzki, C.E. (1983) Process, structure, and world views: towards an integrated view of systemic models in family therapy. *Family Process*, 22, 4, pp.469-576

Shulman, L. (1999) *The Skills of Helping Individuals, Families, Groups, and Communities*. Itasca, Illinois: Peacock Pub. Fourth edition

Thomas, N.D. and Coleman, S. (1997-8) Using the sensory orientation group with a frail elderly population. *Groupwork, 10*, 2, pp.95-106

Ulas, M. and Connor, A. (eds.) *Mental Health and Social Work*. London: Jessica Kingsley

Trevithick, P. (1995) 'Cycling over Everest': Groupwork with depressed women. *Groupwork*, 8, 1, pp.5-33

Wilson, J. (1995) *How to Work with Self-Help Groups*. Aldershot: Ashgate

Yalom, I.D. (1995) *The Theory and Practice of Group Psychotherapy*. (4th ed) New York, Basic Books

Developing the professionals:
Groupwork for health promotion

Ellen E Reverand and Louis B Levy

Many factors influence people's health, and so - promoting their health has to be considered within a broad and complex context. This is why it is necessary to consider the health promotion expertise required of health professionals from different agencies, and how these professionals make sense of their work with each other. In this field, multi-disciplinary groupwork can be used to broaden the expectations of health professionals working across boundaries among agencies, particularly where national and local policy changes appear to make new demands on them. However, such practice is likely to be effective only where a genuinely broad mix of professionals are brought together, and where learning methods address shift of attitudes and not just the acquisition of skills and knowledge.

Groupwork in health promotion is viewed differently by different professions and groups. For example, for some, groupwork means meeting young people in a classroom and telling them to stop smoking. For others, groupwork involves identifying infringements of laws regarding tobacco sales. The former example is often the traditional perception of health promotion. Yet, there is growing recognition of the variety of ways in which health promotion can be effective and of the need to encompass the principles and practices of the latter.

Beattie (1991) describes four ways of working. Firstly, there are interventions that are directed at individuals and are led by the professional. An example of this type of intervention would be a practice nurse encouraging a pregnant woman to stop smoking. In this example, the pregnant woman sees the practice nurse as an expert who has chosen to impart information as a result of observing a practice that has, or is believed to have, a negative impact upon health. Such a form of involvement is directed and initiated by the practice nurse in her professional role and is therefore classified as 'health persuasion'.

Interventions in the second category are once again led by the professional, but in this instance are aimed to protect communities and work more collectively than the style associated with health persuasion. Professionals lobbying for a ban on tobacco advertising would be an example of this category, and this work is described by Beattie as 'legislative or policy action'.

The third category represents that area of work where the professional is focusing on personal development with an individual client. It is assumed here that the health promoter plays a facilitative role and works with the agenda of the individual. An example of this style might include a youth worker helping a young person to identify their health need and then delivering an appropriate intervention. Beattie describes this third way of working as 'personal counselling'.

The fourth way of working is similar to the third category except that it focuses on the group or community level. For example, a local health worker undertakes work with a group of people living in the same area to assist them in identifying their collective health needs. The local health worker then uses their networks locally to involve the decision-makers. This way of working empowers the local community to make decisions about their own health needs and then influence the way action could be undertaken. Beattie describes this area of work as 'community development'.

This article will examine how groupwork with health professionals can be used to help them understand their health promotion roles and work within the context of all four levels.

Before describing our work with the groups, comments about the setting within which the groups are found may be helpful.

Context: The specialist health promotion agency

The work that we will describe in this paper reflects the role of Health First in developing the capacity of others in the local area who have health promoting responsibilities. Health First is a specialist health promotion agency funded through a contract with the Lambeth, Southwark & Lewisham Health Authority (LSL) in London. We are hosted in a Community Trust as a result of the split between providers and purchasers introduced in the National Health Service (NHS) over a decade ago. Health First believes that our specialist services are most effectively used through developing the capacity of others to promote health rather than working directly with the public.

As the specialist health promotion agency in LSL we seek to be at the forefront of innovation and high quality practice in the promotion of health and the prevention of ill health. We are committed to providing quality services that are appropriate, effective and based upon the best available research data - acknowledging the diversity of the communities we serve and recognising the existence of discrimination and oppression which adversely affect their health status. The services we offer take account of the various influences on health and well-being which range from the individual to the socio-economic. Certain principles guide us in our work:

- Acknowledging and respecting the health promotion role of others and seeking to enhance their roles;
- Developing healthy alliances which will work towards improving the health of the communities we serve;
- Recognising staff as the most valuable asset and working together to achieve Health First's maximum potential;
- Upholding and implementing the best practices of equal opportunities in our employment practice.

Health First works with many groups in different settings as illustrated in the middle ring of figure 1. We have developed a range of specialist skills for undertaking our health promoting role and provide these as appropriate for the group(s) with whom we work. Each group is different and hence each combination of

Figure 1

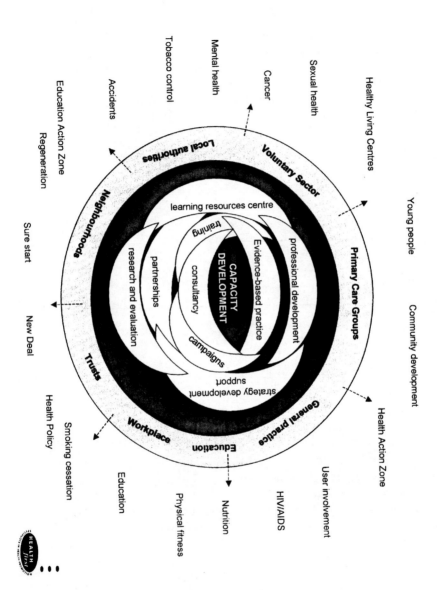

activities is organised to encompass a different range of skills. Such increasing capacity is reflected in the inner circle of figure 1. Often our key area of success relates to our experience and reputation for developing and facilitating partnerships across settings and professional boundaries. It is therefore more likely that our work will involve working across two or more of these settings than within a single setting. For example, Health First is currently working with Primary Care Groups, Community Health Councils, the Health Authority and the voluntary sector to facilitate the development of strategies of involving the public. The outer ring of figure 1 identifies some of the interventions in which we are involved in the local area. These interventions range from the traditional disease areas to the more recently acknowledged wider determinants of ill health, including regeneration issues.

Such work is of benefit at two levels: to the general public, and to those who work with them. This paper focuses on groupwork with the latter, involving work with individuals from fields such as community nursing, workers in the voluntary sector, professionals allied to medicine and the local authority.

With these features of the context in mind, we shall now describe our work with the groups.

'Health Promotion in Practice'

This is the title of a group-based learning intervention that Health First delivers as part of our health promotion role in the local area. The groups develop the capacity of local health professionals and others who have health promoting roles in relation to people in the local community. Each of these individuals, as well as whole professional sectors, has a role to play in influencing the health of the local population.

The influences on the health of the local population range from those factors that are individual to a given person and cannot be changed, such as the genetic features, age, or gender, to those affected by the environment (Whitehead, 1987).

Health First has for some time worked in a multi-disciplinary fashion to bring together professionals from different arenas to learn together about how they can improve their health promotion role. Central to this programme is understanding of how such diverse roles complement each other (Beattie, 1991), and the need to work collaboratively across professional and structural boundaries to achieve the greatest impact on health.

The purpose of this type of learning intervention is multi-levelled. We offer the participants a rich mix of experiences, so they can learn across various settings, and also opportunities to gain formal recognition through accredited learning. In regard to the latter, group members have the option of registering with a local university to achieve academic credits, which contribute to a Diploma in Health Studies should they wish to pursue this later. These opportunities have proved especially attractive for women, for people from the voluntary sector and for those from the ethnic minorities in the local area who may often have experienced disadvantage in the past in relation to gaining qualifications. The programme has a core learning package that can be used in different ways to meet the specific needs of different groups.

What happens in the groups?

To explain how we work we shall use a an example one of the courses we offer—'Health Promotion in Practice'

Group members

Each group on this course will normally comprise between 10 and 16 people who have probably never met each other before. Their common ground is a remit to work with people within Lambeth, Southwark or Lewisham. They may, however, work in very different professional areas and at different levels of responsibility in their own agencies. For example, in the most recent group we had 16 participants. A third were working for the voluntary or community sector, in particular around HIV, sexual health, and with African communities and refugees. Another third were community nurses; that is, practice nurses or health visitors working for the local NHS Community Trust. The remaining third were a mixture of others with a health promoting role, including a chiropodist, a hospital nurse, a social worker, a housing worker and a crêche worker.

Taken together, the range of interventions that these individuals undertook as part of their health promotion roles covered most of the ways of working described in Beattie's model (see above): health persuasion, personal counselling, and community development. In addition there was a distinction between those working in a NHS which is a statutory agency, and those working in community or voluntary sector organisations. That varied membership of the group was typical and reflected our approach to health promotion, as we recognise that a wide range of health professionals have an impact on the health of the local population.

Learning: Organisation, processes and contents

The aim of the 'Health Promotion in Practice' group is to increase the ability of participants to analyse a health promotion intervention in their own work setting. Such analysis includes an emphasis: on a planned programme approach; on the appropriateness of different types of health promotion activities; and on methods of evaluation. These three foci enable the participants to examine systematically how they work with the public to promote health.

Organisation

'Health Promotion in Practice' is delivered twice a year. The programme comprises six days of learning together, organised as three modules. Learning from modules 2 and 3 builds on module 1 which can be seen as the foundation of the course. The rationale for this structure is to allow time between the modules for group members to reflect on their learning while they are back at their workplace. Participants can use this intervening period of independent study to enhance their understanding of the links between theory and practice.

Process

'Health Promotion in Practice' focuses discussion on certain topics by facilitating well known group processes that enable learning about emerging health policies at national and local level. The course utilises active and participatory methods in large and small groups.

The groups allow participants to reflect upon their own practice and that of others - thereby enabling shifts in attitudes and work preferences. These groups are particularly effective for enabling a mix of learning methods which are 'client intensive' - ie. which identify group members' needs – and so have a self-directed component built into them to ensure practical as well as theoretical relevance. We believe that these qualities of the groups enhance skills development and behavioural change by their members.

Working agreements are key to this type of long-term groupwork and time is allocated to developing such agreements at the start of the course. Working agreements are reviewed throughout the three modules, should either group members or facilitators feel this to be appropriate.

This flexible and learner-centred style of groupwork requires intensive involvement by the facilitator - and so, most of the six days are run by two facilitators. One or two core facilitators are there throughout to ensure continuity and facilitate trust in the group, and others are brought in for different sessions to provide specific knowledge around specialist areas such as community development and evaluation. This way of working requires that the core facilitator(s) and visiting experts prepare detailed plans. The design of these plans is based on principles of expected behaviour at different stages of group life (Tuckman, 1965), but it is modified by our experience of what works and what does not. If need be, we also incorporate a range of options for changing the pace and learning methods as we go along. For example, we may find that within one session the level of participants' prior knowledge and confidence varies considerably. In such a case, we divide the whole group into smaller groups and provide them with very different tasks to take account of the differences among them. Such active use of the structure of the group requires that worksheets, checklists and other materials are available to us in case they are needed. However, more often than not, we plan and prepare the sessions 'live': while one facilitator is leading a group discussion, the other is sitting in the corner preparing the next (and very much revised) task. This form of improvisation requires a high level of trust and confidence between the facilitators and can be very rewarding as well as demanding.

Therefore, the facilitators' own support needs must also be addressed. First, the co-facilitators meet together to reflect upon each session and give each other constructive feedback, concentrating on aspects that are normally agreed before the programme commences. Second, there will be several colleagues with similar learning and development roles in Health First, most relevantly in each facilitator's own team, and together they provide an environment where informal support can be accessed within an ethos of safety and shared learning. Finally, Health First has a strong supervision and appraisal framework that provides a formal channel for facilitators to share their successes, concerns and personal development needs.

Choosing the contents

The subjects explored build up and develop throughout the six days, covering the most common range of approaches required for working with colleagues and the public. This range includes: models of health promotion; planning and evaluating work (including setting aims and objectives); current policy changes; community development principles; groupwork; working with individuals; and using leaflets and posters.

As already mentioned, the course is organised as three modules which we shall describe now.

Module 1.   This two day module enables the members to get to know each other, find out how they are going to work together, and discover the breadth of experience from which they will be able to learn; including that of the facilitators and other participants. They are introduced to the notion of health promotion models in the broadest sense - providing an idea of where they and their roles fit into the whole picture of health promotion. There is time to learn about current agendas in health; for example, by looking at new national legislation and local policies. Participants thus gain an understanding of where they, as individuals, fit with the current agendas and policies, and what they can do to have maximum impact in their roles so they work most effectively within the new policies.

From experience we know that, for the participants, the most difficult part of this module is learning to devise concrete aims and objectives for their work. Although the participants are usually very skilled in their ability to work with people, they often find that the area of systematic planning is a new one. Feedback suggests that this part of the module is highly valued by the participants.

Module 2.   Three weeks later the participants return for module 2, which addresses the practical approaches which the participants might use in work with the public. Approaches for community development work are addressed in half a day. This section incorporates principles of involving people in decision making; letting go of some of their power; and a range of different ways of consulting with service users. This part of the module is undertaken in small groups and involves working with real case studies. The beauty of this period is that often participants themselves are a rich source of case studies. We try to be flexible so as to incorporate these experiences into the group's learning. Such sharing has the added value of transforming theory into reality.

Traditionally health promotion has been seen to be about giving the public information through the mass-media. Therefore, during module 2 we spend some time on the role and use of leaflets, posters and displays. Participants are asked to think about criteria to be used in deciding upon the appropriateness of leaflets, posters and displays to promote health. For example, with a poster targeting young gay men's use of condoms the participants would consider when, where and why they might use these materials, when such posters would not be appropriate and the impact that the message would have. Participants also discuss the limitations of simply using leaflets, posters and displays to promote health, and explore other methods of building on these messages resulting in more effective health change.

Following this theoretical review the participants are provided with a first hand demonstration of making effective displays. The opportunity to practice the display of materials for an effective message is then provided, with feedback from other participants as well as the facilitators. We often call this the Blue Peter slot and not surprisingly this always gets a most popular evaluation.

The second day of module two looks at different strategies for directly working with individuals and groups. At this stage in the course it is valuable to draw on the group's experience of working together over the first and second modules. The group is introduced to the stages of group life (Tuckman, 1965), and members are encouraged to reflect upon the different roles individuals take on in groups. Participants rate this topic as invaluable in that it highlights the complexities of groupwork and the different skills and expertise involved in facilitation.

It is at this stage that the assumption that there is a set method of working with individual members of the public is challenged. The assumption encountered is that the most appropriate way to work with members of the public is to tell them that their individual life choices (such as smoking or not practising safer sex) are bad and that giving them information about the detrimental consequences to their health will result in a behaviour change. However it is well documented that such messages are not effective, and that health behaviour change is a complex process (for example, Prochaska & DiClemente, 1986). In-depth discussion of the variety of approaches to support individual members of the public in behaviour change often leads to intense debate and considerable sharing of experiences and learning.

Module 3. A couple of weeks later members come back for the final module which involves: reflection on learning; bringing the learning together; and evaluating the health promotion work that participants undertake. A clear link is made with the difficult work of devising aims and objectives. Participants also have the opportunity of reflecting on the theories covered and linking these practically to their practice. The emphasis is placed upon questions such as 'what has this got to do with me?' and 'what has this got to do with me when I go back to work tomorrow and want to make changes?'

This module is also designed to enable participants to reflect on what they think of the whole course. To this end the facilitators carry out a 'live evaluation' which, while increasing anxiety, is good practice in terms of modelling our own requirement for learning and feedback. The live evaluation consists of the group identifying their own criteria for evaluating the course and its impact upon them. For example, they could decide to comment on the facilitators, on the venue, on the pace of the learning or on the materials used. The facilitators leave the room and the group is required to work in their absence for forty-five minutes. In order to provide some structure the group nominates its own chair, somebody to write up what they are going to decide upon, and somebody to offer feedback to the facilitators. The group presents their feedback, without identifying the source of individual comments for 20-30 minutes while the facilitators listen without interruption. This form of live feedback is combined with a formal evaluation form that the participants complete at the end of each module. After the completion of each course the facilitators prepare an evaluation report that includes the facilitators' own perceptions of the success of the course.

Throughout the three modules, two core themes emerge. One is the issue of equality of opportunity and inequalities in health in Lambeth, Southwark and Lewisham and how best individual health workers can address those issues in their daily practice in a realistic way. The second theme covers the elements of Beattie's model as discussed earlier. We believe that participants come to the course with some idea of their health promotion work as it is at the moment and they leave having a greater understanding of where their role fits within a broader picture. We also hope that participants gain a greater understanding of how they can link with other health promotion workers and structures so that the whole health promotion picture can become more effective in the local area. Part of this outcome is often achieved through the networks that participants may develop on the course itself.

What happens to members after the group ends?

We keep in contact with former participants in several ways. Most usually participants maintain their links with Health First as they feel that the learning has been a powerful experience. Many participants attend other opportunities for individual or group learning, and this enables us to carry out longer-term follow-up, giving us a picture of the relationship between course learning and changes in practice. On the most recent cohort of group members, we have further developed work with three participants as follows.

A chiropodist liaised with one of our facilitators to run a half day session with the chiropodist's colleagues. The aim of this session was to consider how the chiropodists could further develop their health promotion work with clients. The emphasis of this work was to look at the chiropodists as a team in order to consider organising their health promotion work more effectively.

A community worker working with vulnerable women was provided with individual coaching to support her in running a health group with women - something that she had not previously undertaken. In the process of this coaching Health First was able to link this worker with another agency which was able to provide her with premises for her women's group. Additionally, Health First was able to provide her with access to expert input on healthy eating and giving up smoking which the women had themselves identified as a need as a result of the initial work undertaken.

During the course, a practice nurse raised some concerns about the methodologies that the local Health Authority had attempted to employ with local people in a consultation process about services. It was possible for the group facilitator to work with the practice nurse to feed back these concerns to our Health Authority colleagues and investigate different, more appropriate practices which the Health Authority representatives could adopt.

In this way the Health Promotion in Practice group learning is not a discrete intervention divorced from broader development work in Health First. We aim to link in individuals' learning to broader structures and opportunities for networking throughout Lambeth, Southwark and Lewisham.

Emerging themes

Over the last few years we have ran this groupwork intervention on several occasions and three themes come to mind. The first theme relates to the role of groupwork itself. It is clear that for attitudinal shifts to take place, it is necessary for the individuals to interact so as to enable an exploration of feelings, opinions, ideas and values. Structured work in small groups enables members to share feelings, explore moral values (e.g. 'what should health promotion be about?'), analyse real-life case-studies and share their reflections on practice.

The second theme is participants' growing confidence. In particular, their ability to speak in a more informed way with policy makers and indeed their own managers. We find that group members are more likely to make their arguments using evidence and theoretical principles rather than just their own colloquial experiences. This is a powerful means for promoting change in their practice and in the practice of colleagues around them. This level of confidence is likely to be transferred to other areas of the participant's work, therefore having considerable impact upon future practice and competence.

Finally, inter-disciplinary collaboration, is the third theme. As a result of current policies in Britain, health professionals will have to make sense of their own roles through working with others who come from very different backgrounds. To do this, professionals will have to meet together and learn together. Such shared learning is far richer in a group than during private meetings between two different professionals. Therefore, groupwork in health promotion is likely to be a cornerstone for implementation of the government's agenda with respect to public health as noted in *Saving Lives: Our Healthier Nation* (DoH, 1999). Groupwork is clearly linked to the interdisciplinary agenda of partnership to improve health, and the growth of public health, across professional boundaries. Groupwork seems to be part of a shift towards learner-centred learning and sits well within the government's 'third way'. It is likely therefore that group interventions such as Health Promotion in Practice will, for some time, continue to have an important role in local health improvement.

Indicative reading

The following texts reflect the approach Health First has taken both in choosing to deliver this multi-disciplinary group intervention, and in the content of course learning:

Beattie, A. (1991) Knowledge and control in health promotion: A test case for social policy and social theory. in J. Gabe, M. Calnan and M. Bury (eds) *The Sociology of the Health Service.* London: Routledge
Beattie presents a model - a structural grid - mapping the range of ways in which health promotion can happen. This provides a useful tool for enabling practitioners and policy makers to understand the range of factors that influence health, to identify gaps in service provision, and to consider areas where there is a need for individuals and agencies to work collaboratively across organisational and professional boundaries.

Open University (1994) Training and development in a changing world. in. *People and Potential.* Milton Keynes: Open University
This is a learning programme designed to help people with a training and development responsibility to become competent and reflective practitioners. It outlines a range of methodologies for working with learners in groups. More importantly, it considers the role of groupwork within the context of alternative learning approaches.

Department of Health (1999) *Saving Lives: Our healthier nation.* London: HMSO
Saving Lives sets out an agenda for working in partnership across the health economy to improve the life of the population. It is an action plan to tackle poor health and identifies four major areas for work; namely cancer, heart disease and strokes, accidents and suicide. It recognises that improvements in health require a partnership between individuals, communities and the government. It recognises that ill health has many determinants that are complex in nature and include education, employment, environment and life chances.

References

Beattie, A. (1991), Knowledge and control in health promotion: A test case for social policy and social theory. in J. Gabe, M. Calnan and M.

Bury (eds.) *The Sociology of the Health Service.* Routledge, London

Department of Health, (1999) *Saving Lives: Our healthier nation.* London: HMSO

Open University (1994), Training and development in a changing world. in *People and Potential.* Milton Keynes: Open University Press.

Prochaska J. and DiClemente, C.C. (1986) Towards a comprehensive model of change. in Millar and Heather (eds) *Treating Addictive Behaviours: Processes of change.* New York: Plenum

Tuckman P.B.W. (1965) Developmental sequence in small groups. *Psychological Bulletin,* 63, pp.384-399

Whitehead, M. (1987) *The Health Divide: Inequalities in the 1980s.* London: HEC

Groups
addressing social concerns

Learning beyond the classroom:
Groupwork in schools

Marion Silverlock

In the light of 'citizenship' emerging as a National Curriculum requirement and of a long standing employers' discontent with the end product of the education service, two schemes are described here. They illustrate the need for teachers and youth workers to acquire good groupwork skills. Projects are described which indicate the educational gains to be had from 'active citizenship.' The particular skills of the facilitator are outlined and a training model proposed.

Introduction

Among the many current initiatives in secondary education practice are several which try to introduce a real-life element. These approaches are likely to be more attractive and purposeful to students than much traditional classroom work. Prominent among these developments are *student-led* projects, often described as 'active citizenship' or 'community service learning'. In these projects students in secondary schools take the main responsibility for designing and delivering a variety of services to a wide range of people.

Following the publication of the Crick report - 'Education for citizenship and the teaching of democracy in schools' (Sept 98), citizenship will be phased into the National Curriculum over the next two or three years.

Many teachers preparing for the classroom elements of this subject will need help to acquire groupwork and facilitation skills if they are to support active, project-based work beyond the classroom. This skill should be to a level which allows teachers to pass these skills on to students. Because this work is new and evolving, source material for this article is based on fieldwork, whilst current key texts are highlighted in the reading list.

Two schemes stand out as pioneers in this field, offering opportunities to students to directly design and manage projects and then reflect on their learning: Barclays New Futures and Changemakers.

Barclays New Futures

This is one of the largest ever sponsorship schemes in education - £8m was allocated to be spent over 8 years. Barclays gives Awards to secondary schools for projects either in the school or based in the community. The Award includes sustained advisory and evaluation support. Although projects might be initiated and designed by teachers, applicants have to demonstrate how management will be assumed by the pupils. This is a key target of the scheme.

Changemakers

Changemakers in this respect, is a purer model. *All* design, implementation and fund-raising *must* be carried out by young people. This approach is designed for adults working on empowerment or motivation projects with young people. Changemakers publications are included in the bibliography at the end of this chapter.

Students from both schemes are expected to reflect and report on their learning. These new insights can then be incorporated into material for interviews that students attend in applying for jobs. Positive benefits are reported by employers and reflected in comments such as: 'We offered you the job/course place because the way you spoke about your project made you stand out from the crowd.'

The projects

Projects may be in school or out in the wider community. Quite a range is included, for example: peer education - usually older pupils helping younger ones with literacy, numeracy, IT, health education or homework; peer support - teams of pupils specialising in listening and mediation skills, and environmental enhancement - from 'pocket parks' to wetlands management. There are also social projects which, in the South West, include a nationwide network of Young People's Town Councils, a youth radio station, reminiscence projects, arts festivals and support to those with special needs.

Learning outcomes

The educational value of this work increases in direct proportion to the degree of ownership, management and responsibility experienced by the students. Of equal importance is the opportunity for supported reflection, conducted via discussion groups, diaries, feedback and one to one work with a mentor.

When they are given opportunities to present their learning to interested audiences, students tell us that the projects give them insights, skills, experiences and confidence they would be unlikely to gain in any other aspect of school life. A few of their comments may serve to illustrate these claims.

Such thoughtful evaluations emerge when skilled encouragement is employed. To support the process students need to be asked specific, yet open, questions. These questions can be grouped under the broad headings of intellectual, emotional-personal, and social growth, and when students respond to these questions they can be led to the threshold of their own understanding. For example: *What new insights have you gained? Say how you have grown in your ability to take risks. Give an example of your improved teamwork skills.*

Sixth form peer educator: 'I gained in confidence - it helped me to expand myself. I can talk to groups of people and now I know that this is definitely the line I want to take for a career.'
Fifteen year olds, reminiscence project: 'I communicate better with

older people - I've overcome the shock of their mental and physical infirmities in order to listen.'

Fourteen year old young town councillors: 'We took sole responsibility for 200 young people at our conference, so we *had* to make it all work.'

Fifteen year old designers, adapting a sailing boat to carry severely disabled children: 'We studied ergonomics to improve grip and safety.' 'We've given our time and energy and the rewards are as small - or as big - as a smile.'

Thirteen year old arts festival organiser: 'Phoning the bank was a hard thing to do - we were scared.'

Thirteen year old community tutors (history and science): 'We've calmed down a lot and now listen and work as a group.' 'We can handle radio interviews, manage a budget, keep a photographic record and sort out the Press.' ' We can do presentation to VIPs without feeling silly.' 'Now we say we'll have a go - we always used to say no.' 'We amazed ourselves with our good ideas - and we are creating our own web site.'

Further questions lead them to examine their sense of citizenship, their readiness for employment and what benefits there might have been to the school and the community.

The context

Current educational practice and future need.

At present employers complain that our 19th century system of education and training in the U.K. does not produce the raft of experience, skills and self-knowledge they need. Students complain of being talked at, over directed and frustrated. Many adults recall with dismay the irrelevance of much of their schooling. Training institutions give in to the pressure for paper 'evidence' of academic levels of attainment. Skills acquisition suffers from the fragmentation and incoherence generated by over-testing.

Although there are notable exceptions, most schools are not yet producing a majority of pupils who are employable, high achievers, and emotionally competent active citizens. In 1995, Industry in Education published a report, *Towards Employability*, which examined current school and college initiatives. Concluding that even work experience is often too flimsy to be of value, the report found grounds for hope mostly within examples of student-led project work. In 1998, Dr Richard Whitcutt, the organisation's chief executive, reiterated the continuing need for developing teamwork, adaptability, communication and interpersonal skills in young people entering the work place. Speaking at Changemakers conference, he acknowledged the particular value of young person-led projects for the acquisition of these skills and attitudes.

As already indicated, effective learning from student-led project work requires planned time for structured feedback and reflection. To facilitate this process, teachers and youthworkers who are skilled in groupwork techniques would be better able to help teams explore and understand their own growth in some depth. Such enhanced skill is likely to contribute substantially to the linked demands for emotional competence and better planning and execution of tasks in the workforce.

Where are the seeds of essential change?

As such, the Crick report, Barclays New Futures, and Changemakers taken together are powerful signals of change. All three are referred to in current publications by the Department for Education and Employment (DfEE). There are other indicators:

- The Institute for Education, University of London (Dame Pat Collarbone, speaking at a seminar) has strongly suggested that student-led work, including help with the management of the institution, is an indicator of a good or improving school.
- The Education for Citizenship Department of Community Service Volunteers promotes the practice of 'active citizenship' and insists that practical work is student managed and linked with learning outcomes. They want to see this approach

become a vital element within the mainstream curriculum.

- The Prince's Trust - Action has created the Power Millennium Awards Scheme which provides groups of young people with grants of up to £10,000 to develop projects which have a positive impact on the lives of people in their communities. Community Service Volunteers has a similar Millennium Awards Scheme offering awards of up to £6000.

- Most striking of all, £20m has been set aside from the New Opportunities Fund to help schools develop 'study support'; that is, after school activities which enhance both studies and general development. The relevant DfEE document *Extending Opportunities* strongly recommends the value of most extra curricular activity, including community initiatives, and highlights student-led schemes like Changemakers.

Where does groupwork fit in?

Student-led projects normally involve some or all students in management teams. Such groupings range in size from 2-18 participants without losing effectiveness, provided they evolve from the genuine interest and commitment of the young people involved.

Depending on the nature of the project, these teams work on establishing need, solving problems, creating and updating action plans, allocating resources, negotiating with others, raising money, managing budgets, dealing with conflict and celebrating success.

For groups of this nature to succeed, they have to find a way through the minefields of maintenance tasks, emotional interpretation and understanding.

For example, sixth-formers at a Devon rural comprehensive school undertook to deliver the difficult parts of the school's health education curriculum - sexual behaviour and drugs. Working with an appropriate training agency at a seaside hotel they devised, within one weekend, a curriculum for younger (12 - 14 years) pupils. Using role plays, debates, audio-visual displays and lots of energy, this project has run for four years, using successive groups of sixth form volunteers. To succeed, they have had to overcome many initial adult doubts, particularly among teachers. Their younger pupils, interviewed in small groups, failed to produce a negative reaction except, memorably, 'Miss, they might as well shoot all teachers over the age of 25 - they just don't talk our language.'

Such a high risk and visible project made great demands on the group life of the teams. Perhaps had they been conscious of groupwork skills their task might have been more straightforward and coherent.

Broad agreement is now being reached by the key players in the field about what skills are needed to enhance employability and lifelong learning. Changemakers, with the DfEE, have produced a set of worksheets on the enterprise skills required by employers (Garner and Turner, 1999). These bodies have also related employability to learning approaches. Among the 14 enterprise skills are: working effectively in a team, resolving conflict, making decisions, solving problems and giving and taking feedback. How do these skills emerge through self-directing project teams?

The groups at work

Effective team-working is especially necessary where groups of students have to work away from campus e.g. to visit primary schools or retirement homes. Organising the safe movement that this requires introduces students to a number of challenges: logistics, negotiation, maintenance of a wide range of relationships, and a strong sense of personal responsibility - on top of whatever new skills they are evolving through the direct service they are providing e.g. listening, recording, teaching.

When, as usually happens, some members of the team are less committed than others, then fury flies (the stage of storming) and it is at this early stage that some skilled facilitation is useful. An insightful teacher might be able to hold the group together, but it is not uncommon for some groups to shrink in size quite rapidly, without any real understanding of the reasons.

Decision making is at the heart of the empowerment process -

real decisions, not just choices from options selected by others of higher status. This process can become more 'real' than is anticipated: one group, with a simple plan to create a pocket park for the community out of a scrap of waste land, found themselves at the mercy of a careless property developer. Aged 13, they decided to 'get political', approached all the residents in nearby new housing and in less than a month had set up a Community Association which went on to do battle over telephone boxes, shops and play areas. I have a treasured memory of a white faced 13 year old boy making his first ever phone call to the House of Commons to enlist the support of his local Member of Parliament - watched in terror and admiration by the rest of his team. This process contributed in equal measure to widening the students' horizon and to group bonding.

Problem solving is also built into task-based group processes and may range from dealing with simple logistics to handling outright opposition. A group who wanted to carry out some simple wetlands conservation work on someone else's land found themselves treated as the enemy by the landowners as well as the property developer. The landowner was hoping to sell his illegally drained land to the local authority architects who said they had decided to build a classroom block on the school campus site. The group subsequently elected to go for an alternative pond project, but, as they did not have enough enemies, the electricity company announced that the third chosen site would prevent mains connection to the new building. Opposition and problems like this are rare but contain much learning for a group which is expertly facilitated through the reflection process.

The giving and taking of feedback is intrinsic to this process. Group members are asked to make positive comments on each other's successes and new skills, and treat what might be seen as 'failures' as just another problem to be solved. Typically, groups of young people are shy of positive comment and outspoken with negative remarks. The special value of structured reflection in this situation is the opportunity to draw learning from every aspect of the overall experience, including the experiences of conflicts.

Sessions of this nature are organised with every group towards the end of their two year projects with Barclays New Futures. Most groups delight in talking about their period of conflicts, seeing it more in the light of an episode in a soap opera than as an integral part of group process. A skilled and insightful groupwork facilitator can greatly enhance the learning outcomes from these exciting moments.

So what help do teachers need to gain such skills?

Training teachers in groupwork skills

Teachers and youthworkers need space and time to explore the implications of this approach to learning and to draw on their own experiences of working in effective and ineffective groups. What special skills do the group facilitators need?

Skilled groupworkers in this context are able to:

1. listen actively and with respect. Many adults merely wait for the opportunity to put in their own ideas, without giving serious consideration to the views of the young people, and are often anxious to impose solutions which are safe and acceptable to adults. The willingness of a facilitator to wait and listen enables the group members to argue their way towards solutions which are often equally acceptable to adults. This open-minded listening can be demonstrated by posture, facial expression, small signals of approval and other conscious and creative uses of body language.

2. Create space for each group member to contribute. Regardless of whether the facilitator is also the chair, s/he can model concern to hear from everyone and ensure that each member leaves the exercise feeling useful, included and valued.

3. Allow emotion and the expression of feelings. It is not usual to hear adults in education admitting that emotions are what drive people, often despite our attempts to be rational. A strong emotion, given permission to show itself, acknowledged and perhaps even valued, immediately loses

much of its power to damage. For example, young people quickly learn to apply the questions 'how is this useful and how is this not useful, to the group and how can we profit from it?' Through these questions they absorb the vital principle that our rational thinking can be enhanced by a willingness to learn from and integrate the expression of emotion.

4. Coach in conflict resolution. These techniques can be introduced to even very young children with spectacular results. Highfield Primary School, serving a poor estate in Plymouth, has turned itself around by introducing and rewarding democratic processes such as:

'Circle Time - where we discuss all our problems and sort them out',
'Guardian Angels, who fly to your rescue when you're being bullied or if you need help', and
'A school council which works with every campus adult to make school a safe, pleasing and fun environment.'

In the event of dispute, Highfield children understand that there is always more than one valid point of view, that much bad behaviour is based on fear and that rational discussion, where everyone gives way a little, can lead to the resolution of conflict.

Elsewhere older children, like those at The Royal Manor School in Portland, develop mediation skills, involving work with bullies and their victims. Mediators come from all years and only seek the help of staff if they feel unable to cope. Teachers need to be able to coach groups in these techniques if these are to be applied consistently as part of the educational process.

5. Encourage task and leadership sharing and the clarification of goals and values. It has been saddening to watch some project teams struggling with loss of direction, loss of impetus and unequal workloads when the task seems too difficult.

Groupwork skills introduced early on would have saved and enhanced these projects.

Is training needed?

It is not unusual for teachers and youthworkers to claim that they are already working in this way. Some can accept the principle of student-led learning, but may not be able to give the necessary support. Failure to set up structured reflection or examine process may leave students little wiser about teamwork. Under pressures of time, budgets, unsympathetic accounting systems and long experience of being the principal decision maker, many well intentioned professionals revert to a directive style or to finding it more expedient to do things themselves. Supporting student initiatives can seem risky and time consuming by comparison. Consistency of support is crucial, but it is not easy for teachers to perform both authoritative and facilitative roles with equal success. Specific skills training, particularly that which would draw on their own experience of good facilitation and of empowerment, would help more adults working in education to understand and value young person-led learning.

A training model

Discussions with teachers and leading proponents of young person-led learning suggest that groupwork skills training for teachers should be local, affordable and based on one session per week. A weekly, supervised, experiential group session can be supplemented by a personal learning journal and a short reading and research list. The learning can be structured as a 'spiral curriculum' similar to the one year counselling course model approved by the South West Open College Network and built around the learning needs of the individuals involved. Accreditation should be an added option.

A course might look like this:

Duration: Three terms of 10 weekly, 2-3 hours group meetings.

Session contents: sharing of personal experiences of facilitation and empowerment; exploration of negotiation; shared leadership; giving and taking of feedback; the life cycle of groups; creative conflict; collaborative problem solving; power and influence; roles and functions; body language; task and maintenance skills.

Added to this would be the particular facilitation skills listed earlier: active and respectful listening, creating space for all group members to contribute, handling emotion, conflict resolution and clarifying values.

There would also be time to discuss the application of these skills in the school environment. Role-play adds fun and illuminates this exploration. Teachers' classroom experiments with groupwork would provide further material that can be examined.

Training methods used would include brief inputs, whole group and small group discussion, as well as goldfish bowls (one small group works in the centre of the room, watched by an outer circle of observers, who add their observations to the review process which follows).

Between and after sessions, reflections on new learning or the difficulties encountered can be recorded in the personal diary. Material from these notes can be presented for discussion voluntarily during group sessions.

Reading and research should include background documents on active citizenship and Net searches for relevant material, as well as standard groupwork texts.

Assessment should be by a mixture of self, group and tutor evaluations, involving peer and tutor discussions and referring to personal journals. These processes, taken together, will provide further material for the whole group. An external evaluator should check and maintain overall standards.

The creation and delivery of such a course should employ groupwork specialists acting as tutors and facilitators. Teachers, youthworkers and other specialists should advise on form, content and accreditation of such courses.

There is likely to be a proliferation of new training opportunities as the citizenship concept gathers momentum. So, there is a real danger that classroom content ('civics') and organisation will predominate and that skill development for teachers will be omitted, as it is time consuming and more demanding of the assessment process.

The role of all professional supporters of learning is already beginning to shift away from that based on information and position power. Society and employers need young people with high standards of problem solving behaviour, based on self-esteem that is itself based on worthwhile experiences of managing real life issues. Educators need space and time to consider the role of groupwork in helping teachers to meet that target.

Indicative reading

Bentley, T. (1998) *Learning Beyond the Classroom. Education for a changing world.* London: Routledge
A wide ranging review of educational innovations in the UK and an analysis of current economic, social and technological change which shows the need for radical reform of the way we think about young people's learning. It points the way ahead to a new role for schools as brokers of education and is sympathetic to student-led learning that involves a wider community.

Department for Education and Employment (1998) *Extending Opportunity: A national framework for study support.* London: DfEE Publications Centre
The case for learning outside school hours with special mention of self-directed learning through schemes like Changemakers.

Garner, S. and Turner, D. (1999) *Enhancing the Enterprise Skills: Supporting young people in shaping their futures.* London: DfEE Publications Centre
A set of workbooks for teachers and youth workers, designed to help with the facilitation of young person-led activities. The authors describe a role wider than that of groupworker, encompassing information and resource gathering. The integral worksheets may be attractive to both students, teachers and youth workers for mainstream work, study support and informal, small groupwork.

Bibliography

Corey, G and Corey, M. (1982) *Groups: Process and practice.* Belmont, California: Brooks/Cole

CSV. (1998) *Active schools: Citizenship through Active learning in the community.* A CSV Occasional Paper with Barclays New Futures

Garner, H. (1993) *Multiple Intelligences: The theory in practice.* New York, Basic Books

Goleman, D. (1998) *Working with Emotional Intelligence.* Canada and USA: Bantam

Industry in Education. (1995) *Towards Employability. Addressing the gap between young people's qualities and employer's recruitment needs.* London: Industry in Education

Johnson, D. and Johnson, F. (1987) *Joining Together: Group theory and group skills.* New Jersey: Prentice-Hall

Leadbeater, C. (1997) *The Rise of the Social Entrepreneur.* Paper No. 25, London: Demos

Leadbeater, C. and Goss, S. (1998) *Civic Entrepreneurship.* London: Demos/Public Management Foundation

Leigh, A. and Maynard, M. (1997) *Leading Your Team.* London: Nicholas Brealey

Mitchell, P. (1998) *Education for Citizenship: The contribution of active learning in the community.* London: CSV Education for Citizenship

Potter, J. (1998) *Citizenship Education and the Role of Local Government.* Briefing Paper No. 4. London: CSV Education for Citizenship

Advisory Group on Citizenship (1998) *Education for citizenship and the teaching of democracy in schools.* (The Crick Report). London: Qualifications and Curriculum Authority

Silverlock, L. and Silverlock, M. (1995) *Teachers, learning, ego and groups.* Groupwork, 8. 2

Evolving the curriculum:
Groupwork and community based learning

Lynne Muir

Community based learning has developed in a range of settings, where people take an active part in identifying what they want to find out and how they can acquire this knowledge. In this chapter, the various approaches to community based learning will be described, and the major debates reviewed. The growing emphasis on life-long learning, where objectives are set by learners and continuously revised by them as relationships develop in the group, will be highlighted.

Who participates?

Community based learning includes opportunities to gain more understanding and skills through various group experiences - some formal, and others more informal. These informal learning situations usually have an educational (Jarvis, 1995), rather than a therapeutic (Hayden et al., 1999) or preventative focus, but the methods of work have some features in common. This type of group work can take place in many different settings, for example: facilitating a group of residents to establish a new community or youth centre; working with parents in the community who are liaising with a junior school to create a joint 'learning to read' programme; 'empowering' ethnic minority groups to press for separate leisure facilities and linking colleges to the community through a range of developmental activities. Some of these activities are described more specifically later in this paper. Because community based learning develops in various contexts, a number of models describe these experiences.

Major models

Ian Martin (1987) identified three major models used for working with community groups: the universal, the reformist and the radical.

The universal approach

The *universal* approach is a top down method of working which is familiar to all from formal educational settings. Groupwork conducted within formal education is characterised by pre-determined membership, professional leadership, structure and topic-based group discussion/seminars. These types of group also exist within the social work setting, with anger management and alcohol abuse groups run by the probation service, as prime examples.

The reformist approach

The *reformist* approach is adopted where certain groups of people are identified as needing special help. The Educational Priority Area Projects of the 1970s provide a large-scale example of this model. Selected areas had resources poured into them for a limited period of time. One critic of these projects; Steve Baron (1989), considered that identifying certain groups as vulnerable (e.g. single parents, black people) separated them from the rest of the community. It remains, however, a popular way of working in situations where resources are limited and choices must be made - social work groups, probation groups and some youth groups are often based on the same premise.

The probation service has a long history of developing targeted groupwork services, such as parenting skills groups for mothers on probation orders and communication skills groups for young offenders in prison. The programmes are usually fairly flexible, with opportunities for the participants to identify specific areas of difficulty and develop ways of resolving them. There are also many youth work projects where workers link with young people in the community and, using groupwork methods, jointly fashion objectives and take action to achieve them. One London project, with two detached workers, operates in the open community with disaffected adolescents and has incorporated the Achievement Awards scheme into their work (Marchant, 1999). These examples clearly fit within the reformist style of community based learning.

The radical model

The *radical* model was made famous by Saul Alinsky (1970) who worked with groups picketing factories, notably Kodak. In those circumstances the slogan 'the end justifies the means' had real teeth. This method is often used outside formal organizations by residents' groups who withhold rent or maintenance charges until change is instituted, or who picket Whitehall to protest at the closure of a local hospital. Local leadership will often help to coordinate these groups.

Paulo Freire's claim that education constitutes a political act informs the radical view. In his extensive writings, Freire, a South American educator, fostered the notion of empowerment (Freire, 1970). He believed that education was a joint struggle by educators and educatees (his word) to critically understand their circumstances, so that they became better able to order their world and thus move closer to fulfilling their potential (Allman and Wallis, 1997). He restated his original ideas from the 1960s on a visit to London in the early 1990s, when he said that he was not a non-directive facilitator but an active resource for the group with whom he was working. This pro-active view of the groupworker's role in community based learning has been developed by others. The Scottish Adult Learning Project used Freirean ideas, as well as groupwork methods in a community based setting (Kirkwood, 1991).

Although many group workers would see themselves as practitioners of the radical model, I believe most are actually universal and reformist practitioners - both in education and in social work. It is difficult for workers to loosen the control exerted through a 'top down' approach, as both social work agencies and educational institutions often have a 'message' to impart. Radical methods are seldom used within formal organizations as workers may find themselves unemployed if they rock the boat too fiercely.

Despite the examples, these three models are not fully adopted by everybody as there are different perceptions and practices within the field.

Major debates

Advocates of community education and community based learning both see education as a process which is life-long, in which participants are actively and influentially involved and in which the needs of the participants determine the nature and timing of provision (McConnell, 1996). Many writers use the terms 'community education' and 'community based learning' interchangeably, but others would see clear differences between these two approaches. Originally, 'community education' was seen as providing learning opportunities in which the content to be assimilated was determined in advance. In 'community based learning' the content tended to arise out of discussion amongst the learners.

Clark (1996) defines curriculum and curriculum development as an organized learning process. For the community curriculum to be the focus of community education, it must be set within a community school or other agency where it can be fostered and developed. Clark's pedagogic model is based on providing education - but he would define education as drawing out and moving on, not moulding and shaping.

The development of links between formal and informal learning has been explored by Bentley (1998), who writes of a curriculum for a life-long learning community that is constantly changing as the participants respond to the current reality. For McConnell (1996), 'community education' covers the work done in schools and colleges, social work, leisure and recreation departments, the prison service, industrial bodies and local and national voluntary organizations, institutions whose main aims are not primarily educational.

'Community education' was the term used in the 1970s and

1980s for work conducted across boundaries between schools and their local communities. Work targeted primarily within a community, with no links to established organizations, tended to be defined as 'community development'. In the 1990s, the term 'community based learning' gained wider usage. The growth of open learning networks, the encouragement by the government of the concept of life-long learning (at the same time as it was cutting support funding) and the general acknowledgment that learning does not just take place within formal organizations, strengthened the use of the community based learning terminology. There was also a general recognition that participants came from many different settings including housing associations, community police and the health services. Community based learning information is now available on the internet.

One group, Cobalt, has its own definition. They believe that community based learning (CBL) is about learning that is assessed as part of a student's degree, and that CBL Teamwork

is about any method of student learning which takes them outside of the university or college, into the community, to learn from that experience. (Cobalt, 1999)

The Cobalt project is looking at country-wide examples of community based learning in order to identify and disseminate information on examples of good practice. Indeed, community based education has been extended into some courses of higher education. There are now sixty-three projects funded by the Higher Education Funding Council.

These differences in the definition of what community based learning covers have been both frustrating and challenging. The debates have revealed a lack of conceptual clarity, but also an openness to new ideas and projects. The concept can encompass a wide field (McConnell, 1996), or can be narrow (Cobalt, 1994). But whatever the definition, all categories of workers require a wide range of skills and knowledge, a pre-eminent example of which is groupwork.

However, while there are some differences in definition, most writers would see community education and community based learning as open systems which involve the whole person in exploring new areas. In this sense, all these approaches are forms of groupwork.

The role of groupwork

David Clark (1996) is a writer in the community based learning field who is also familiar with groupwork methods and has a model of practice closely linked to the approach. He defines the community educator as one who works on the boundaries between systems, seeking to create and develop learning communities. He sees the primary role as that of an educator using the skills of agent, facilitator, coordinator, manager, team leader or network resource. His intervention cycle sees the community educator acting as a connector to the various aspects of working with groups such as making approaches, forming alliances, looking at alternatives, facilitating access, encouraging action and appraising the outcome.

All of these steps would also be present in groupwork practised in other settings. However, Clark's approach differs from that of some other community based workers, in that he believes, as discussed earlier in this paper, that a community educator must work from the basis of a curriculum and that too much deviation waters down the impact of the work. While some groupworkers operate from a stated base or curriculum, many would try to work in partnership with the community, developing a focus based on their emerging needs and working towards objectives which are periodically reviewed and reformulated.

The emphasis throughout the 1990s has been on the recognition that academic and vocational qualifications should be equally valued, that objectives should be clearly identified and that the emphasis should be on learning, rather than teaching (Jackson, 1995). Lack of motivation and confidence can deter people from engaging in vocational courses, but there is some evidence that participation undertaken as citizens or residents brings a liberating sense of increased confidence (Elsdon, 1994). This point is also illustrated in a study by Seru (1997).

Current examples of community based learning

At present community based learning seems to incorporate influences from many of the strands discussed before. Examples of good practice have been extensively documented and encouraged by Colin Fletcher (Broad & Fletcher, 1993), who has stressed the importance of setting clear objectives and evaluating achievements. The lack of these has long been the Achilles' heel of groupworkers who have operated on a rear view mirror principle: they know where they have been but do not know where they are going (Bloom, 1975). This sharpening of practice skills can only enhance groupwork and give it the credibility it has lacked.

One of the advantages of students doing a degree in community based learning is that they need to have clear objectives, research methods and evaluation of those methods in writing up their dissertation or project. As they are usually carrying out a project at the same time as they are researching it, their practice improves.

SHARE, a family learning project designed to contribute to the quality of parents' involvement in their children's learning, is one example of a community based learning programme. This is run from infant/primary schools and coordinated by CEDC (the national centre for community-based learning). Through the use of groups, teachers act as facilitators in helping parents understand how children learn and providing them with activities to use at home with their own child. The process also gives parents an opportunity to discover their own abilities. Parents can participate in the groups with or without assessment, but if they choose to be assessed, the scheme is run through the Open College Network.

Another project based on group work methods was run in the community with no formal education links. Meadow Way is a densely populated community of 350 properties, with a population of 1250 (half of whom are under 16 years of age). There is high unemployment (20%), disproportionate numbers of single parent households, overcrowding and low car ownership. The community is located on the outskirts of an affluent Home Counties commuter belt. There were no standard amenities (no shops, cafe, post-office, church, or out-of-hours bus service). A group of residents decided to address the problem and held jumble sales to raise money to buy four secondhand portacabins. They gradually fitted them out and although no grant was given, they did have the ground rent waived, until an elected member complained that the project was being 'wet-nursed', resulting in the ground rent being reinstated. The community worker, who was looking to develop some evaluation criteria for her degree, used her networking and groupwork skills to obtain a grant of £10,000 to repair the portacabin roofs and provide technical assistance. The residents learned how to use tools, design shutters, install insulation, interpret plans and make presentations to businesses, councillors and other groups. They reviewed their constitution and achieved charity status so they could apply for lottery funding. The project offered opportunities for community based learning and a 'community in the centre' rather than a 'centre in the community'. (Fletcher, in Allen et al, 1987). The community worker held several focus groups with the members and evaluated their assessment of their own learning. Their reponses can be summarised in this example:

'We get there by pooling ideas and going around the problem to find another solution, if ever we are stuck for an answer', and 'we've become more flexible and now know who to ask and what questions to ask'.

This is surely a good example of practice based research graphically illustrating the learning experienced by community members, facilitated by the groupwork skills of the researcher.

A further example illustrates the transferability of skills from one culture to another using groupwork skills in a community based setting. A worker from CEDC went out to Jordan to carry out a needs analysis survey in the Palestinian camps. She decided to establish a group of adolescent trainers whom she would train, so that they could go into the camps and recruit further groups, replicating the process she had used. She recruited a group of ten (aged between nine and twenty years of age) and used flip charts with open ended questions, raising issues such as: 'what is this community?' 'what changes are there on the horizon?' and 'which are positive and which negative?' The main difficulty in implementing this community based learning exercise was not in enthusing the young people, but in restraining the staff from taking it over from them. Each adolescent trainer recruited a group of five or six, carried out the exercise and then fed the information back to the worker for compilation and assessment. The ability to apply the skills learned increased both the confidence and the knowledge pool in the local residents.

The University of the Third Age is an informal network of people who share their knowledge and skills with peers in a variety of settings. Some share their knowledge of playing bridge on the London to Cambridge commuter train. Another group is dedicated to saving a wide range of little known apples, and a third meets regularly to read and discuss Jane Austen. All these groups are examples of life-long learning.

The concept of life-long learning is integral to community based learning and one that all practitioners should encourage. So, in practice terms, I am back where I began: working with groups using a learning framework in a community setting. Perhaps T.S. Elliot's (1942) words convey this best:

We shall not cease from exploration
And the end of all our exploring
Will be to arrive where we started
And know the place for the first time.

Indicative reading

Bentley, T. (1998) *Learning beyond the Classroom: Education for a changing world.* London: Routledge

Clark, D. (1996) *Schools as Learning Communities.* London: Cassell

Jarvis, P. (1995) *Adults and Continuing Education: Theory and practice.* (2nd Ed) London: Croom Helm

Reference

Alinsky, S. (1971) *Rules for Radicals*. London: Housmans

Allman, P. and Wallis, J. (1997) Paulo Freire: An appreciafion. *Adults Learning*, May, p.233

Baron, S. (1989) Community education: From the Cam to the Rea. in S. Walker and L. Baron (eds) *Politics and the Processes of Schooling*. Milton Keynes: Open University

Bentley, T. (1998) *Learning Beyond the Classroom: Education for a changing world*. London: Routledge

Bloom, M. (1975) *The Paradox of Helping*. Chichester: John Wiley

Broad, B. and Fletcher, C. (eds) (1993) *Practitioner Social Work Research in Action*. London: Whiting and Birch

Capper, L. (1998) *Share. Teachers' Handbook*. Coventry: CEDC

Clark, D. (1996) *Schools as Learning Communities*. London: Cassell

Cobalt (1999) http://www.bham.ac.uk/CoBalVcbl.htm

Eliot, T.S.(1942) Little Gidding

Elsdon, K. (1994) Values and learning in voluntary organizations. Conference paper at the University of Nottingham Department of Adult Education, Feb. 22

Fletcher, C. (1987) The meaning of 'community'. in G. Allen, J. Bastiani, I. Martin and K. Richards (eds) *Community Education: An agenda for educational reform*. Milton Keynes: Open University Press

Freire, P. (1970) *Pedagogy of the Oppressed*. Harmondsworth: Penguin

Hayden, A., Hopkinson, J., Sengendo, J. and Von Rabenau, E. (1999) 'It ain't (just) what you do, it's the way that you do it'. *Groupwork*, 11, 1, pp.41 -53

Jackson, K. (1995) Popular education and the state: A new look at the community debate. in M. Mayo and J. Thompson (eds.) *Adult Learning, Critical Intelligence and Social Change*. Leicester: NIACE

Jarvis, P. (1995) *Adult and Continuing Education. Theory and practice*. (2nd Ed) London: Croom Helm

Kirkwood, G (1991) Education in the community fallacy: 'The community educator should be a nondirective facilitator', in B. O'Hagan (ed.) *The Charnwood Papers, Fallacies in Community Education*, Education Now

Longworth, N. and Davies, W.K. (1996) *Lifelong Learning*. London: Kogan Page

Marchant, H. (1999) Personal Communication

Martin, l. (1987) Community education: Towards a theoretical analysis.

in G. Allen, J. Bastiani, I. Martin and K. Richards (eds) *Community Education: An agenda for educational reform*. Milton Keynes: Open University Press

McConnell, C. (ed.) (1996) *The Making of an Empowering Profession*. Edinburgh: Scottish Community Education Council

Seru, L. (1997) *Towards an Understanding of Community Education Practice in the Local Government Setting Using Case-studies of Downside and Meadow Way Estates to Test the Effectiveness of a Model of Evaluation*. Unpublished dissertation for the M.Ed. in the Practice of Community Education. Coventry: CEDC/University of Warwick.

Breaking the culture of silence:
Groupwork and community development

Jacky Drysdale and Rod Purcell

This chapter introduces the reader to the principles and actions of community development, through one of the principal methods; groupwork. It does this by offering one case example of the groupwork aspects of a community development group. This example is set in the context of the growing importance of a community development approach to meeting current political imperatives; such as combating social exclusion, working in partnership with communities (either of interest or geography), and promoting participation within the political and democratic processes. Some reflections are offered on the history of community development and its value base. Community development seeks to challenge oppressions and encourage people to be vocal and active in identifying their own concerns and seeking appropriate solutions for them.

The here and now

Since the mid 1990s community development has been undergoing a rediscovery in the United Kingdom. The turning point was marked by a speech given by Virginia Bottomley, then Secretary of State for Heritage in September 1996. That speech recognised the significance of the social exclusion of citizens, and the need to reverse this trend through partnerships with communities.

From May 1997 many UK Government speeches (see for

example, Blair, 1997) and policies have placed social inclusion at their heart. They acknowledge the need to support communities in relating with government and agencies (HMSO, 1999a), to encourage proactive self-help, and recognise the importance of personal growth and learning throughout the life cycle for all citizens (Cmd.4048). This is clear in the health sector from the document 'Our Healthier Nation' (Cmd.3854 and Cmd.4269) and the development of Healthy Living Centres and Health Actions Zones.

In the social and economic spheres the community development process requires local involvement in rural and urban regeneration bids (Social Inclusion Partnerships and Single Regeneration Budget programmes). The process contributes to environmental sustainability through, for example, the implementation of local Agenda 21 initiatives; These initiatives support sustainable development as a result of Chapter 28 of Agenda 21, the United Nation's sustainable development action plan for the 21st century, which was agreed at the Earth Summit in Rio de Janeiro in 1992. The process is also part of community safety initiatives, the development of housing associations and housing co-operatives, of issues relating to community planning and the decentralisation of government, and of planning for real and community care (HMSO, 1998.). Overall, community development is concerned with the promotion of active citizenship.

In the late 1990s then, community development is practiced in diverse settings under a wide variety of names across the community, voluntary and local authority sectors (CoSLA 1990; Purcell 1998; Barr, Drysdale and Henderson 1997). Community development is no longer the province of a group of community workers. It has become a method of working for social welfare organisations, housing agencies, health service workers, health promotion workers, educators, economic development workers, town and country planners and ecologists who seek to promote change in partnership with communities. This expansion necessitates a clear understanding of the approach and clear links to other skills located within the training and experience of these professions. Groupwork may be one of these generic skills.

One example of a community development group

Tuckman (1965) produced a model that explores the development process of a group, through the stages of 'Forming', 'Storming', 'Norming' and 'Performing'. The model was later elaborated to include a 'Mourning' stage. As with all groups (Whitaker, 1985), community development groups start by encouraging individuals to interact with each other, by learning skills and increasing knowledge about themselves and each other, by establishing moods and atmospheres. In community development these stages encourage the development of personal empowerment and ensuring that action is taken to challenge oppressive practices.

The processes involved can be illustrated by examining the establishment of a drugs forum through a community council and a community health project in a Scottish town (see Barr, Drysdale and Henderson, 1997). A group of local residents on a housing estate expressed concerns about the increase of drug use after a young person had died. The community council and the community health project joined forces to acknowledge the visibility of drug use in the area. They discussed with agencies and politicians what local people could do to reduce drug misuse. Some of the people were already experienced community activists, and they managed to recruit a variety of other local people who were parents or who had an interest in the issue. This was the 'forming' phase of the group. Forming is when the group members are preoccupied with getting involved and being included.

In general people will become engaged with community development groups for a number of reasons (Henderson and Thomas, 1992) which may alter with time:

• to protect their personal and/or family interests;
• for social and cultural activities and support;
• to improve the quality of life within their community;
• to preserve or create community assets;
• to examine opportunities or repel threats whether real or perceived.

For this community group there were aspects of protecting family interests, improving the quality of life in the area and repelling a threat. Through the action of meeting together as a group, and with the support of a community worker, people began to recognise a common interest and to reach a contract for group action. When people began to critically evaluate themselves and their social situation, they gave credence to the possibility of change, which enabled them to build confidence and assertiveness over time.

However, to reach this point the people involved had to deal with the stage of storming. During this process people tested out themselves and other people in the group. Roles were sought or rejected, and power was a significant dynamic. The initial view expressed by the group was that the identification and expulsion of drug dealers, who lived locally, would solve the problem. This view exposed many differences of understanding, of values and of attitudes within the group. As is often the case during this stage, people also made some irrelevant contributions, as group norms were not yet established. Yet the debate generated some frank discussions and highlighted the need to try to establish what would be a fair and just response.

On further investigation, and as a result of researching the experiences of other neighbourhoods, the initiative was rejected as ineffective. Clearly through that difficult stage of seeking cohesion, shared were strong enough to enable networking and discussions with other interest groups. The role of the worker in supporting and facilitating the group through these difficult times was crucial. This role reflects the experiences of groupwork writers such as Schwartz (1961), Shulman (1984), Douglas (1976) and Doel and Sawdon (1999). During that phase the group had to respond to prejudices relating to young people, drug users, rival territories and attitudes towards agencies and services. Members needed to disclose their views and have their ideas and prejudices challenged. The group needed to increase their awareness, knowledge and skills about the real issues.

Then came the 'norming' phase of the group's development. During 'norming' a culture of trust and belonging developed. A belief system emerged that, though not entirely consensual, could be sanctioned by everyone. The group established and enforced policies of equal opportunities, and later, when they received funding to employ staff, made stringent efforts to ensure that local people had equal opportunities to be appointed to the jobs. Through the storming and norming stages issues of dealing with oppression were made central to the work of the group.

The phase of the group where thoughts and ideas were translated into tangible actions (performing) came when the group improved its networks within the community. The tasks were focused and the group began to function effectively. The group started to expand its membership by including a wider range of people. They established a community organisation and publicised it in the area. They visited local schools and youth organisations. They exchanged information and ideas with local agencies and with other people concerned with drug misuse in the area. From this phase clear outputs and outcomes emerged. The members also wanted to work with young people in extending their access to, and knowledge of, a drug free lifestyle. To this end a workshop that involved local people and agencies in mutual learning, and managed to develop a partnership that could have some impact on the problem they had defined.

The workshop was a great success and the 'performing' stage was in full flow. The group also instigated a local drug forum. They worked in partnership with local voluntary and statutory agencies to identify gaps in the services, including a needle exchange point to reduce the numbers of needles found in the street. They worked with families, neighbours and friends around the apprehension of having this exchange clinic situated on the estate, by highlighting the benefits, and monitoring the difficulties. They received a small grant to develop an 'Alternative to Drugs Programme' for drug users in the area. One night each week users who were drug free got involved in other activities and in peer support. These activities involved appointing, training and managing staff, and accountability for budgets.

We would like to emphasise that the group process was not a linear experience: Indeed workers changed, members left and were replaced and so various aspects of 'mourning' were experienced. The fact that a bid to become a partner in the development of a local drug team failed was a particular low point. Yet after each set back the common objectives could be revisited. A struggle similar to storming followed, but a consensus for joint work was re-established.

In community development terms such stages of group development are needed to create strong community organisations, and enable the participation of local people in political and democratic power relationships.

For the drug forum, the ability to influence policy and practice followed soon after the conference. The drug forum became influential, and was invited to work closely with health staff, social work staff and the voluntary agencies to develop policy and practice in the locality. This could have been the final phase of the community development process when people begin to understand how to use their own power to influence policy and practice. However, in community development the process continues so that achievements are sustainable. Therefore, while there are often transitions and changes, endings are less frequently encountered than in other forms of groupwork.

What is community development?

Community development is the underpinning theory of community work practice and has a long history in the UK. Its nature and purpose has changed over time (for fuller discussion, see the community development writer Popple; 1995).

> It is an approach which strengthens local democracy and the capacity and voice of communities to participate actively in determining the process and outcomes of social and economic change. A range of professionals and agencies can adopt this approach. (Scottish Community Work Forum, 1994)

The beginnings of community development can be traced back to two discrete foundations, 'benevolent altruism' (such as that associated with Victorians like John Ruskin) and grass roots community action. The first influence came through the working men's educational institutions of the 19th century, the early

University settlements and various self help schemes developed amongst the poor of the Victorian era (Jacobs and Popple, 1994; Craig and Mayo, 1995).

From the 1920s onward community associations were developed around social and cultural activities, particularly on the inter-war housing estates. Much of the focus of this work was centred on social, educational and leisure activities. However, it was in the post war era that community development as we recognise it today began to fully take shape. The transfer to independence of the former British colonies throughout the 1950s and 1960s led to the return to the UK of community development workers who had been instrumental in building local administrations for independence. Alongside this in the 1960s was the growth of a more grass roots based radical practice in working class communities, for example the squatters movement and campaigns around housing (O'Malley, 1977; Radford, 1970).

The Community Development Projects from the late 1960s and 1970s, were funded by the Home Office, and attempted to tackle pockets of urban poverty. These projects developed a political, economic and structural critique of poverty (see: CDP inter-project editorial team, 1977). Many people have argued that they failed to develop a linked model of practice (Loney, 1983; Waddington, 1983). Yet throughout the 1970s and early 1980s practice became increasingly incorporated into local government activity through urban programme funding, the growth of the Youth and Community Service in England, the Community Education Service in Scotland and the movement in some authorities towards community social work practice (Cockburn, 1977; Barclay Report, 1982).

From the mid 1980s onwards community development was affected by a number of other influences. Firstly, feminist theory (Hanmer and Rose, 1980; Rowbotham, 1992) and practice were adopted by community development workers. This led to consideration of gender, process and personal politics. Secondly, the ethnic minority communities highlighted issues of race and culture alongside the traditional class analysis of community development (Sivanandan, 1990). Simultaneously community development became a victim of local authority funding cuts and of the Thatcher dictum that rejected the whole notion of society. The Major and now the Blair administrations have begun to reverse this decline.

Various contemporary definitions of community development have been put forward by various bodies such as the Association of Metropolitan Authorities, Voluntary Activities Unit of the Home Office, Combat Poverty Agency in Ireland, Federation of Community Work Training (see Barr, Hashegan & Purcell, 1996). They all have the following principles in common. Community development:

- involves promoting change;
- seeks to challenge social exclusion and promote full citizenship;
- is anti discriminatory in its outlook, and practice;
- encourages empowerment of individuals and groups through increased participation in decision making;
- has an educative function in relation to the community and the organisations which work with those communities;
- seeks to collectivise and develop new forms of association and organisation.

If the values and principles above tell you what community development aims to do, the next question is how it achieves this. In October 1996, the Scottish Community Development Centre completed research commissioned by the DHSS in Northern Ireland. That project produced a report that provided a functional analysis of the dimensions and elements that were necessary for a community development process to be claimed (Barr, Hashegan & Purcell, 1996). The process involved four core dimensions:

1. Personal empowerment;
2. Positive action;
3. Community Organisation;
4. Power relationships and participation.

These dimensions are interrelated and should be viewed as a 'checklist' to decide to what extent community development is taking place. It is however important to have some idea about the practical manifestations of these rather abstract terms.

These elements reflect the values and purposes of community development highlighted above. In addition the model requires

1. Personal empowerment	2. Positive action
• the development of informal skills and knowledge (through the community development activity) by local people • formal or non formal training and education about the purpose of the activity, or the process of working • a conscious belief in the possibility of change • development of leadership within the community.	• understanding of needs in relation to discrimination • existence of equal opportunity policies • evidence of equal opportunities practice • affirmation and assertion of cultural heritage and identity
3. Development of community organisations	4. Power relationships and participation
• investigation and monitoring of community needs • nature of the recorded activities run by community organisations • levels of activity in community organisations • support networks between people/ community organisations in the community	• openness and accountability of community organisations • understanding of policy frameworks and political systems • effective influence by community organisations on public policy or practice

the outputs and outcomes of community development to be identified and measured in both quantitative and qualitative terms. These outputs and outcomes relate largely to the degree of *empowerment* at individual, family, group and community levels and the changes in the *quality of people's lives.*

Community development and groupwork

Promoting change that combats social exclusion and discriminatory attitudes and practice cannot solely be an individual activity. Oppressive conditions and discrimination originate within institutional and cultural levels of society.

Changing these requires individual personal growth, but its success lies in the ability to generate effective organisations that can challenge institutions, agencies and governments, and create movement in terms of understanding, policy and practice. This is the logical conclusion of ideas developed by groupworkers such as the 'mutual aid system' proposed by Scwhartz (1961, p.7-34) or Lee's 'empowerment group approach' (1994, p.208-261).

Mutual aid and empowerment necessitate mutual learning experiences by citizens in terms of the rights and responsibilities of their citizenship and by governments in terms of recognising and responding to people's experiences and aspirations. As Lee (1999) wrote:

> The very existence of the group provides potential for personal and political empowerment and for strengthening and restoring human connection. (Lee, 1999, p.8)

Community development is a change activity. It seeks to galvanise people who are disadvantaged or excluded to examine their experiences and commonalties and to determine and prioritise their needs. Through this process people are enabled to organise around their common needs. This animation of people can be in a geographical location or around issues or experiences that motivate people to take action.

In community development, perhaps more sharply than in some forms of groupwork, there should be clear outputs (products of the action; e.g. establishing drug advice services) and outcomes (effects of the action; e.g. change in drug use patterns). The process that facilitates this also receives significant attention. There are both individual and group components, but community development is founded on the principle that the medium of collective action is essential:

> ... that every human being, ... is capable of looking critically at his world in a dialogical encounter with others. Provided with the proper tools for this encounter, he can gradually perceive his personal and social reality as well as the contradictions in it, become conscious of his own perception of that reality and deal critically with it. (Schull, 1972 in Freire, 1972, p 8)

For community development to take place it is not enough just to be aware of the group dynamics and the stages 'forming – storming – norming –performing -mourning'. Workers need also to understand the personal development experienced by group members and assist the group to focus on the essential tasks that need to be pursued if change is to be achieved. Community development happens almost exclusively in groups. However, this does not mean that groupwork theories are acknowledged or practised effectively. When groupwork is used as the principal method of promoting community development, there is a clear awareness of the personal level, and of group dynamics; there is a clear plan and process for change, and mutual learning is identified and acknowledged. The authors have called this 'community development groupwork'.

The personal and task-oriented aspects of community development groupwork can be explained through the work of Freire (1972 and 1974) and Henderson and Thomas (1992). The diagram overleaf illustrates the overlap of these activities.

Paulo Freire (1972; 1974) has explored how groupwork techniques can help people develop their critical understanding of themselves and their life. Freire's approach is used widely in the developing world and his approach also works well in the UK. It can be applied to any group setting.

Freire argues that the role of the worker in the group setting is to act as a facilitator. The worker in a community development context should not be leading the group to a predetermined end, but enable group members to gain a greater understanding of their personal, family and community situation. For this to happen group members have to develop a more critical level of consciousness. Lee (1994) uses many quotes and ideas from Freire and his three main levels of consciousness to explore both individual and groupwork practice. These are explained below.

Firstly, there is '*Magical Consciousness*' when people accept the oppressions of external powerful forces; they do not fully comprehend the socio-economic or other social contradictions that exist in our world. They do not believe in the possibility of change because they are caught in the '*Culture of Silence*'. Such

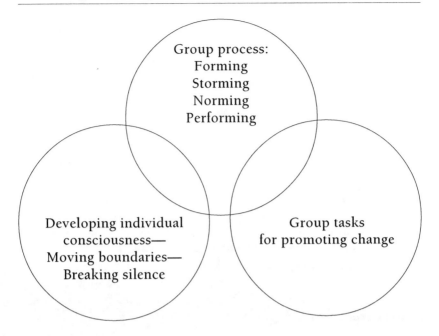

Group process:
Forming
Storming
Norming
Performing

Developing individual
consciousness—
Moving boundaries—
Breaking silence

Group tasks
for promoting change

silence can operate at a community level, for example in a community living in substandard housing, where there are few job opportunities and where schooling and health services are inadequate. Magical consciousness also operates at the personal level, for example among women subject to domestic violence who feel trapped and where their suffering is unheard and unacknowledged.

Freire defines the next level as 'Naïve Consciousness'. This is where people can reflect on their situation and begin to make connections with social, economic and political issues. However, the worldview at this level is very much one of individualised experience. For example, the non-availability of good housing may be blamed on single parents or the shortage of jobs on immigrants. At this level issues are subject to simplistic analysis and emotional responses often with other social groups being classified as deserving or undeserving.

The major step of viewing life through 'Critical Consciousness' does not come until people engage with the context of the outside world on an analytical basis. The impact of structural and cultural discrimination is understood, and problems move from being private troubles to becoming public issues (C. Wright Mills, 1959). It is essential to the community development process that the object of the work and activities are generated by the group themselves as a result of this process of consciousness development.

Related to these levels of consciousness is Freire's concept of *'Boundary Situations'*. He contends that we all repress ourselves through imposing a boundary on our own actions as a result of internalising the cultural norms of oppressive institutions and belief systems. Through using a problem posing technique, the groupworker should facilitate the group to question these assumptions, to develop a more critical view of themselves and their community and shift their self defined boundaries. If this expansion of boundaries is achieved, belief in the possibility of change becomes conceivable. The group is then able to move from the *Reflective* phase to developing a *Vision* of a better personal and collective future, and go forward to *Plan* and undertake *Action* to these ends.

Henderson and Thomas (1992) developed a model that outlines the various tasks each community development group has to accomplish to effectively promote change. These tasks can be identified as:

- Making contacts and people coming together;
- Forming and building an organisation;
- Clarify goals and priorities;
- Keeping the organisation going;
- Dealing with friends and enemies;
- Leavings and endings.

The processes that lead to accomplishing these tasks are not necessarily linear. Community development groups often work over a long period of time. After all, promoting change is never easy. The group may loose and recruit members constantly throughout its life. The group may also have a number of successes as well as failures. The ability to sustain group activity through the highs and lows requires particular skills and awareness on the part of the groupworker.

Conclusion

Success in community development groupwork involves working on multiple processes simultaneously. The process involved in the stages of forming, storming, norming and performing are common to many groups. In addition the development of group members' critical understanding of themselves and the wider group tasks is necessary. As these processes unfold, changes in the aims, purposes and activities of the group can be expected (Mullender & Ward, 1991; Lee 1994; 1999). The challenge for the groupworker is to understand these multiple processes and to facilitate their progression. The reward is the empowerment of individuals with collective strength and cohesion to contribute to positive change in their communities; to break the 'culture of silence' and promote a more active exchange between policy makers and citizens. Achieving this shift may convert the rhetoric of current policies into the reality of an improved quality of life for ordinary people.

Three major sources

We include for further reference, three diverse approaches to undertaking groupwork in community development settings:

Lee, J.A.B. (1994) *The Empowerment Approach to Social Work Practice.* New York. Columbia University Press.

This is an excellent example of using a community development approach to working with individuals and groups of people. While Lee does not overtly use the term community development, her work follows closely the value base of community development by trying to find ways to deal with oppression and 'seek liberation' for people in poverty or those experiencing social welfare difficulties

Hope, A and Timmel, S. (1995) *Training for Transformation.* (3 volumes) Zimbabwe: Mambo Press

This is a practical book that provides many accessible exercises for the application of Freire's work to groups. Book 1 focuses on the basic method and the reflection and vision stages. Book 2 is concerned with group dynamics, developing leadership and participation, decision making, planning and evaluation. Book 3 looks at linking global issues to the local context and how to develop local trainers and workshops.

Henderson, P. and Thomas, D, (1992) *Skills in Neighbourhood Work.* London: Routledge
The book takes an implicit pluralist approach with the focus very much on working within a neighbourhood. It is valuable as a 'how to do it' guide. Each of the chapters provides a thoughtful range of issues to be considered by the groupworker. For those who are new to working with community groups this book will prove to be indispensable

References

Agazarian,Y. and Peters, R. (1981) *The Visible and Invisible Group: Two perspectives on group psychotherapy and group process.* London: Routledge & Kegan Paul

Barclay, P. (1982) *Social workers: their role and tasks: The report of a working party ; set up in October 1980 at the request of the Secretary of State for Social Services by the National Institute for Social Work; under the chairmanship of Peter M. Barclay.* London: National Institute for Social Work

Barr, A, Hashegan, S. and Purcell, (1996) *Monitoring and Evaluation of Community Development in Northern Ireland.* Belfast: Voluntary Activity Unit. DHSS

Barr, A., Drysdale, J. and Henderson, P. (1997) *Towards Caring Communities.* Brighton: Pavilion

Benjamin J., Bessant, J. and Watts, R. (1997) *Making Groups Work. Rethinking practice.* St. Leonards, Australia: Allen and Unwin.

CDP Inter-Project Editorial Team (1977) *Guilding the Ghetto. The state and poverty experiments.* (Cmd 3854) London: HMSO

Cockburn, C. (1977) *The Local State.* London: Pluto Press.

CoSLA (1990) *Recommendations for the Way Forward in the Identification of Standards Linked to Vocational Qualifications: Community work feasibility study.* London: Care Sector Consortium, Voluntary Organisations Group

Craig, G. and Mayo, M. (1995) Community Empowerment: A reader in participation and development. Atlantic Highlands, NJ: Zed Books

Doel, M. and Sawdon, C. (1999) *Teaching and Learning Creative Groupwork*. London. Jessica Kingsley

Douglas, T. (1976) *Groupwork Practice*. London. Tavistock.

Douglas, T. (1983) *Groups: Understanding people gathered together*. London. Routledge

Freire, P. (1972) *Education: The Practice of freedom*. London, Writers and Readers Publishing Co-operative

Freire, P. (1974) *Pedagogy of the Oppressed*. Harmondsworth: Penguin

Hanmer, J. and Rose, H. (1980) Making sense of theory. in P. Henderson, D. Jones and D.N. Thomas (eds) *The Boundaries of Change in Community Work*. London: Allen and Unwin

Henderson, P. and Thomas, D. (1992) *Skills in Neighbourhood Work*. (2nd ed). London: Routledge.

HMSO (1998) *Working Together for Healthier Scotland: A consultation document*. 1998. (Cmd 4048). Edinburgh: HMSO

HMSO (1998) *Opportunity Scotland: A paper on life long learning*. Edinburgh: HMSO

HMSO (1998) *Modernising Community Care: An Action Plan*. London: HMSO

HMSO (1999a) *Bringing Britain Together: A national strategy for neighbourhood renewal*. London: HMSO

HMSO (1999b) *Towards a Healthier Scotland*. Edinburgh: HMSO

Hope, A, and Timmel, S. (1995) *Training for Transformation*. (3 volumes) Zimbabwe: Mambo Press.

Jacobs, S. and Popple, K. (1994) (eds.) *Community Work in the 1990s*. Nottingham: Spokesman

Lee, J.A.B. (1994) *The Empowerment Approach to Social Work Practice*. New York: Columbia University Press.

Lee, J.A.B. (1999) Crossing bridges: Groupwork in Guyana. *Groupwork*, 11,1, pp.6-23

Loney, M. (1983) . *Community against Government: The British Community Development Project 1968-78*. London: Heinemann Educational

Mills, C.W. (1959) *The Sociological Imagination*. Harmondsworth: Pelican

Mullender, A, and Ward, D. (1992) *Self-Directed Groupwork: Users take action for empowerment*. London: Whiting and Birch

O'Malley, J. (1977) *The Politics of Community Action*. Nottingham:

Bertrand Russell Peace Foundation

Popple, K. (1995) *Analysing Community Work: Its theory and practice.* Buckingham: Open University Press.

Purcell, R. (1998) *Mapping of the Community Work Occupational Domain to Research Potential Numbers for the N/SVQ.* Sheffield: Community Work Forum

Radford, J. (1970) From King Hill to the Squatting Association. in A. Lapping (ed) *Community Action.* (Fabian Tract 400) London: Fabian Society

Rowbotham, S. (1992) *Women and Movement: Feminism and social action.* London: Routledge

Schull, R (1972). Forward to *Pedagogy of the Oppressed* by Paulo Freire. Penguin: Harmondsworth

Schwartz, W. (1961) The social worker in the group. in *New Perspectives on Services to Groups: Theory, organisation, practice.* New York: National Association of Social Workers.

Scottish Community Work Forum (1994). Edinburgh: Scottish Community Education Council

Shulman, L. (1984) *The Skills of Helping Individuals and Groups.* (2nd ed) New York: Columbia University Press

Sivanandan, A. (1990) *Communities of Resistance: Writings on black struggles for socialism.* London: Verso

Touraine, A. (1981) *The Voice and the Eye. An analysis of social movements.* Cambridge: Cambridge University Press

Tuckman, B.W. (1965) Developmental sequence in small groups. *Psychological Bulletin*, 63, pp.384-99

Waddington, P. (1983) Looking Ahead- Community work in the 1980s in D.N. Thomas (ed) *Community Work in the Eighties.* London: NISW

Whitaker, D. (1985) *Using Groups to Help People.* London: Routledge

Values as Context:
Groupwork and social action

Mark Harrison and Dave Ward

This chapter outlines the history and theoretical foundations of social action. Social action is a values-led approach to practice in which groupwork is a key element of the model. This relationship, however, brings into focus recent trends in groupwork practice which, it is suggested, merit critical reflection among groupwork exponents. Examples of three areas of social action activity are described: practice, training and research; and the paper concludes with a critical discussion suggesting lines for further development.

The social action approach

Social action emerged in the late 1970s and early 1980s as a distinctive approach to empowerment and was located initially in work with young people at risk and in trouble (Ward, 1979; 1981; 1982; Harrison et al, 198;, Burley, 1982; Fleming et al, 1983). It was first conceptualised in detail as 'Self-Directed Groupwork' (Mullender and Ward, 1991) which Payne (1997, p.280) describes as offering 'a clear view empowerment theory focused on groupwork settings and processes.'.

Social action has been developed reflexively and in partnership by practitioners, service users and academics in the course of developing, carrying out, and evaluating interventions, training programmes and action-research. The approach has been recognised as applicable in a wide range of human service settings and to have wide currency internationally (Breton, 1994; Brown,

1996; Jakobsson, 1995; Lee, 1994; Treu et al, 1993). Besides Britain, social action work is currently taking place in projects in eastern and western Europe, North America, and Australasia. *Self-Directed Groupwork* (Mullender and Ward, 1991) has been translated in full into Ukrainian (1996) and in summary into French (1992). Many social action workers and participants link up through the Centre for social action at De Montfort University in Leicester (UK) and share experiences at the Centre's annual international summer school.

Social action has two central characteristics. Firstly, it rejects the 'deficit' and 'victim blaming' approaches which dominate social welfare, promoting instead a commitment to the capacity of all people to take action to improve the circumstances of their lives. Secondly it bases this action on a process of open participation in which people, working collectively in groups, explore the underlying social issues effecting their everyday lives as the foundation for action. Practitioners do not lead but through a non-elitist, highly skilled process, facilitate group members in making choices and taking action for themselves.

Through a continuing and reflexive process of practice and debate among workers and service users, a set of six key principles has developed which provides an adaptable framework for social action practice in a range of settings: training (eg Ward, 1989; Canton et al, 1996), research (eg Ward, 1996/7; Dyson and Harrison, 1998; Fleming et al, forthcoming) as well as practice. These are:

Refusing to accept negative labels: all people have skills and understanding on which they can draw to tackle the problems they face. Professionals should not attach negative labels to service users.

The right to chose and control: all people have rights, including the right to be heard, the right to define issues facing them, and the right to take action on their own behalf.

Complex problems: individuals in difficulty are often confronted by complex issues rooted in social policy, the environment and the economy. Responses to them should reflect this understanding.

Collective power: people acting collectively can be powerful.

People who lack power and influence can gain it through working together in groups. Practice should reflect this understanding.
Workers as facilitators: *methods of working should reflect non elitist principles. Workers do not lead but facilitate members in making decisions for themselves and controlling whatever outcome ensues. Though special skills and knowledge are employed, these do not accord privilege and are not solely the province of workers.*
Tackling all forms of oppression: *social action workers will strive to challenge inequality and discrimination in relation to race, gender, sexual orientation, age, class, disability or any other form of social differentiation.*

These principles have been graphically expressed in cartoon by Muldoon (1994/5) reproduced opposite; and James (1997, p.7) succinctly summarises the shift in perception they involve:

Problems	⟶	Solutions
Deficits	⟶	Assets
Clients	⟶	Citizen Decision Makers
Objects	⟶	Subjects
Problems in	⟶	Problems rooted in
Individuals		Systems

Theoretical and practical inspiration for social action comes from the work of Paulo Freire (1972) and the challenge has been to apply his ideas in working, initially in the UK but, subsequently, more widely afield, most notably in some of the former communist states of eastern Europe. (Mullender and Ward, 1992; 1996; Fleming and Keenan, 1998). Social action holds much in common with the theory and practice of community development. Here the challenge is to adapt the values and practice developed in collective action on structural issues from the predominantly locality based context of community work and working with 'ordinary' albeit poor people, to the more fragmented and specialist concerns of social work. Social action has been influenced strongly by the struggles of the disability movement (see for example: Oliver, 1992), black activists and writers (see for example: Cress-Welsing, 1991; hooks, 1992; Ahmed, 1990;

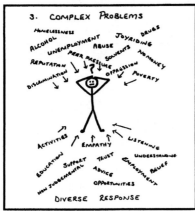

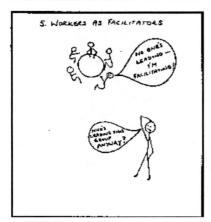

and Gilroy, 1987) and the women's movement (see for example Hudson, 1989; Dominelli and McLoed, 1989; Langan and Day, 1992; and Evans, 1994). They indicate the complex way in which various dimensions of exclusion and oppression are distinctive but still interlink. Each overarches the others at different times and in particular conditions, requiring independent action but within a coherent world-view. Methods developed in social education and in social skills training are adapted for the exploration of issues and the preparation, implementation and evaluation of action. (See Mullender and Ward, 1991, for the methodology set out in full.)

This formulation of social action differs from the normal usage of the term in North America, where generally it refers to a range of forms of

> professional effort to bring into public discourse issues which, according to the consensus between power holders and the public, should remain in the shadow of public debate. (Staub-Bernasconi, 1991, p.36)

social action is practice and activity which are committed to social change and social justice. (Breton, 1995). While this generic definition still appertains, the focus of this paper is upon social action as an explicitly articulated practice theory and methodology which is making a prime contribution to debates about empowerment and associated working practices (Adams, 1996; Payne, 1997; Barry, 1996; Barry et al, 1998/99; and Fleming et al, 1998 in response). Groupwork is central to social action and these practices.

Why Groupwork?

Whether one takes the generic or the narrower approach to social action, groupwork is at the heart of practice. In the American context a special volume of the journal *Social Work with Groups* (Vinik and Levin, 1991) has been devoted to the inextricability of the connection:

The group has been recognised as a social microcosm in which its members can be helped to become participants and leaders in social action through experience with the group process and through engaging in social action processes in the group's immediate social environment. (Shapiro, 1991, p.8)

American groupwork writers vary widely in how they interpret this. For many, taking a pluralistic view of social relationships, this means groups providing an arena in which competing interests might be mediated and integrated. In so far as interpersonal relationships reflect social relations within the broader social structure, groups provide a training ground for democracy and can contribute to the common good. (Shapiro, ibid). However, there are American groupworkers (for example: Breton, 1994; Lee, 1994) who, while placing the group at the centre of social action, take a more radical stance and ground their practice on principles which resonate strongly with those set out above. As Shapiro (1991, p.19) puts it: 'They recognise that not only the personal is political; practice is also political'.

Returning to our starting point in the work of Freire, groups are both the 'context' and 'instrument' of his *Pedagogy of the Oppressed*. This is because in groups personal troubles can be translated into common concerns. In groups the experience of being with other people in the same position can engender strength and new hope where there was apathy before. In groups a sense of personal responsibility internalised as self-blame can find new productive outlets. Alternative explanations and new options for change and improvement can be opened up. The demoralising isolation of private misfortune can be replaced in the course of working together with a new sense of self confidence and potency, as well as concrete gains, which individuals on their own could not contemplate. (Mullender and Ward, 1991, p.12).

But this could be read as groups and groupwork providing merely 'technical support' to some greater enterprise. We would argue that it is much more than just this. Besides achieving material changes and raising the confidence of their members, groupwork has *transformative* capacity. Mistry's (1989) description of a group for black and white women is a classic example of how groupwork, where affiliated to empowerment, can be tremendously powerful in moving people towards more humane and emancipatory relationships. So, bearing this in mind, what has distinguished groupwork, historically, from other forms of practice and connects it to social action, has been:

> an emphasis on the commonalities of problems and situations _.In groupwork each issue that is raised, even when that issue at first glance seems to have no relevance to others in the group, does have applicability for all. The worker who practices *real* groupwork draws out that applicability and elicits the commonalities and asks members to examine the issues of others. (Kurland and Salmon, 1993, p.10, my emphasis)

In such groupwork groups develop lives of their own, over which the worker cannot have complete control; the agenda can be holistic and the process open and inclusive. Group members raise what is important to them, no matter what ground rules and boundaries have been set. It has been argued elsewhere (Ward, 1998) that such free-flowing characteristics are out of kilter with the current climate of social work with a resultant emphasis on structured groupwork 'programmes' with predefined purposes, audited outcomes, discipline and a focus on the individual, in fact *work-in-groups* rather than groupwork.

It is *real* groupwork that is at the heart of social action, groupwork which can align with 'concepts of equality and democracy' (Douglas, 1993, p.31) and which is 'anti-oppressive in its context, purpose, method, group relationships and behaviour'. (Brown, 1996, p.83).

Social action live

Practice

Butler (1994) writes in this journal about a social action group for women whose children were adjudged by social services as at risk of significant harm from their parents. It took place in a family centre run by a national voluntary agency, facilitated by a part-time social action groupworker. Butler, who was asked to evaluate the work of the centre, describes how social action groupwork engendered an atmosphere of equality, enabling the women 'to explore the humour, sadness and strains of family life and no longer remain silent about these.' (Butler, 1994, p.178). Central to the group agenda emerged structural dilemmas facing members: women's sexuality and their relationships with male partners, which were entangled with the processes of racism and the difficulties of bringing up mixed-parentage children. Faced with relentless hardships, the women easily identified the nature of the politics of poverty. The opportunity the group provided to unpack structural and individual issues was critical to these women's empowerment and the creation of their own solutions to the threats and dilemmas they faced. (Butler, 1994, p.163).

Training

A team of social action trainers has been undertaking training for youth social workers in Ukraine. (Fleming and Keenan, 1998). Groupwork is central to the training process. The trainers made it very clear that they had not come with solutions to Ukrainian problems. They offered the social action framework but the actual content was to be the participants'. Courses were run in three cities: Kyiv, Kharkiv, and Odessa, for workers in three districts. They were experiential, group-based and all the exercises and techniques used on the course could be used with groups of young people in the field. Each course had three parts. The first was a week long visit from two trainers and focused on the identification of problems facing young people, exploring their causes, examining different models of intervention, identifying the values base they wanted to work to and developing ideas for working in partnership with young people to address specific issues they face. The last session of this week was spent drawing up action plans. The second part encompassed the next six months during which participants attempted to put their action plans into practice and to use their learning from the course in their work, using each other for advice and support. The third and final part was a another visit from the trainers to review progress, and to reflect on and share the learning, among the whole group, from what had actually happened in the work.

Projects which the Ukrainian youth social workers have developed in partnership with young people with whom they worked included: new initiatives in 'Reform Schools', groups of disabled people enabling them to have a greater say in what happens to them, work with the police, contacting and working with 'street children', work with young men and young women on issues surrounding relationships and on violence, self-help groups for young parents.

This approach elicited a very positive response from course participants. Feedback in course evaluations included:

> The atmosphere of the course - mutual support and understanding - this was very helpful in order to do creative and productive work.

> The method of planning was very useful ... working out programmes ... the scheme of social action ... the methods of identifying problems young people may have.

Research

Here the example is a Health Needs Assessment commissioned by a Health Forum within a large urban regeneration agency. (Fleming, 1997). The brief was to obtain detailed information, to supplement an earlier quantitative survey, of the views of people living in the area about the quality of their lives from a health perspective and to generate ideas for actions to improve residents' health. Although not entirely group based, groupwork made an essential contribution to the research process. (See also Ward, 1996/7, for further examples.)

Adapting the social action practice model, the research team began by asking local residents and professionals, 'What are the questions we should be asking people about their health?'; 'Who should we be asking?'; 'How can we find the answers to these questions?'. It emerged that the concept of health had different meanings for different people. Local people, generally, did not see health in medical terms. They talked about 'happiness', 'satisfaction', 'energy levels', and 'being able to do all you need to do in a day'. It was agreed to use the term 'health and well-being'.

Based on these discussions, semi-structured interviews asked people individually and in groups about *what* factors they thought effected their health and well-being; *why* they thought these factors existed; and *how* they thought matters could be improved. People identified many and varied issues. Health and well-being was seen as benefiting from the support of family and friends, getting together with people like themselves and, for those that had them, jobs and financial security. Conversely, poor housing, financial worries, racism fear of crime, lack of appropriate cultural and linguistic facilities, poor environment and pollution, poor transport and mobility problems, and unemployment were said to adversely effect health.

However, the researchers were very aware of Oliver's observation (1992, p.105) that the experience of being researched can be isolating, reinforcing the dominant idea of problems being individual. Thus, meeting respondents in groups where they could bounce ideas off each other and develop ideas further was a major aspect of the project. Some of the groups were existing groups where people already knew each other and discussed things together, for example, a group of Polish elders at a social club. Others came together especially for the research, for example, a group of older Muslim men who all attended the Pakistani Centre for lunch but had not worked as a group before. Members of this group expressed common issues: difficulties in getting interpreters, poor housing, the need for adaptations for physically impaired elders. They came to realise they were not alone with their problems and identified action others could try out.

Another example of the power of group activity in this research comes from a group young Muslim women with children. Through taking part in the study they identified loneliness and isolation as very real problems which, for them, adversely effected their feelings of well being and thus their health. They decided they wanted to organise regular meetings for themselves and their children. They negotiated with Pakistani Community Centre to use the centre on the day the men were at the mosque and lobbied for recognition and funding from the local authority.

The debate continues

The potential of groupwork framed within social action principles has been highlighted by these examples. However it is important to acknowledge that social action and its roots in Freire's pedagogy has some strong critics. Points made are that social action raises unrealistic expectations about changing the world. It reifies process and leaves real problems of 'managing to survive day to day, finding a job and/or constructive activities and support networks rarely defined'. (Barry et al, 1998/99, p.68). In so doing, critics argue, it promotes action that inadvertently gives more legitimacy to, rather than questions, the existing social order (Barry, 1996, p.7). Further, it is asserted that social action, no less than any other 'method', represents an imposed worker-led agenda which in the final analysis serves the interests of the professionals at the expense of the poor and excluded. (Page, 1992; Baistow, 1994).

These are serious and challenging questions. However, they can be addressed at two levels, the practical and conceptual, and through this thinking it might be that further directions for practice can be offered. First, at the practical level, the examples presented to back up critique are invariably drawn from practice which does not follow the methodology. (see Barry, 1996, and Fleming et al, 1998, in response). In contrast, the examples above show how social action work, which has engaged people in the process of working in partnership on an open and transparent agenda, can achieve tangible material gains countering exclusion and alienation.

Second, criticism of the applicability of Freire's pedagogy leads into a debate of a different order. The point made is that Freire's work belongs to 'another time and another place':

[It is a] ... treatise on educating revolutionaries in oppressed countries about the need to similarly educate, politicise, and revolutionise the

> people ... In societies which are highly polarised such as Brazil, a wholly
> radical agenda may be the preferred route. However, in societies such as
> the UK, despite some stark extremes, more diverse agendas might be
> more appropriate. (Barry et al, 1998/99, p.67, p.69)

First, a misapprehension must be corrected. Freire wrote his
major works while living in the USA, where he 'found that
repression and exclusion of the poor from power were not limited
to developing countries and changed his definition of 'third
world' to a political rather than a geographical concept.' (Branford,
1997, p.19). Second, such thinking reflects a 'dualistic' view of
the social world (Layder, 1994). It sets the 'third world' against
the developed world as if what applies in one cannot do so in the
other. Recent events in Europe surely show that boundaries are
not so clear cut. Likewise process is set against product; big
problems against little ones; changing society against joining it;
worker against participant. In contrast social action, following
Giddens (1984), adopts a non-dualistic position, taking the view
that people are shaped by the world around them but they are also
creative agents capable of effecting the shape of that world (Ward,
1982, p.4). All people, even the subordinated, are never
completely powerless in situations (Foucault, 1980); they have
some means in their control to influence and change things. Non-
dualist practice requires 'sociological imagination' (Wright Mills,
1970), rising above either/or explanations. This means for
groupworkers a *holistic* concern for members as people and for
the issues they confront in the world in which they live. The
group is both context for, and instrument of, personal and social
change (Douglas, 1993). The agenda could not be more
demanding nor diverse.

Such 'joined-up' thinking is also at the heart of current
Government policy, the search for regeneration through *The
Third Way* (Giddens, 1998). It recognises that tackling structural
problems is a key feature of tackling poverty and exclusion and so
enabling people to mobilise their creative potential. Undoubtedly
it is crucial that the right volume and quality of concrete resources
are put in and are targeted to the right places. However, it is clear
that this will not automatically liberate peoples capacities to find

new and better solutions. What also is needed is a process that will effectively 'join up' the 'New Deal' programmes with people in need. Our experience is that many are sceptical, demotivated and, indeed, understate and devalue their potential. This is not surprising, given the social experiences and economic conditions that many have had to endure under the market-centred policies and the unrelenting 'survival of the fittest' rhetoric of the past 20 years. Social action, with groupwork at its core, addresses the necessary connections between people and policies. It does not provide a panacea but, we would argue, it does ask some of the essential questions and has demonstrated enough success, in the most unpromising of circumstances, to have the right to be taken seriously.

Further reading

Lavalette, M., Penketh,L. and Jones, C. (eds.) (1998) *Anti Racism and Social Welfare*. Aldershot: Ashgate.
This edited collection contains two papers on different aspects of Social Action in an anti racist context. One chapter is on involving community members as 'researchers" and bringing about changes in service provision (Dyson and Harrison). The other chapter is on developing a community based child protection service through Social Action (Fleming and Wattley).

Mullender, A. and Ward, D. (1991) *Self Directed Groupwork: Users take action for empowerment*. London: Whiting and Birch.
This text presents in details a methodology for Social Action groupwork.

Shera, W. and Wells, L. (eds.) (1999) *Empowerment Practice in Social Work: Developing richer conceptual foundations*. Toronto: Canadian Scholars' Press.
This volume brings together some of the latest thinking from around the world about empowerment practice. A chapter on Social Action research from the Centre for Social Action (Ward and Fleming) is included.

References

Adams, R. (1996) *Social Work and Empowerment*. London: Macmillan

Ahmed, B. (1990) *Black Perspectives in Social Work*. Birmingham: Venture Press

Baistow, K. (1994) Liberation or regulation? Some paradoxes of empowerment. *Critical Social Policy*, 42, pp.34-46

Barry, M. (1996) The empowering process: Leading from behind? *Youth and Policy*, 54, pp1-12

Barry, M., Davies, A. and Williamson, H. (1998/99) An open response to the concerns of the Centre for Social Action in Issue No.60. *Youth and Policy*, 62, pp.67-70

Branford, S. (1997) Word power to the poor. *The Guardian*, May 10th, p.19

Breton, M. (1994) On the meaning of empowerment and empowerment-oriented social work practice. *Social Work with Groups*, 17, 3, pp.23-37

Breton, M. (1995) The potential for social action in groups. *Social Work with Groups*, 18, 2/3, pp.5-13

Brown, A. (1996) Groupwork into the future: Some personal reflections. *Groupwork*, 9, 1, pp.80-96

Burley, D. (1982) *Starting Blocks*. Leicester: National Youth Bureau

Butler, S. (1994) 'All I've got in my purse is mothballs.' The social action women's group. *Groupwork*, 7(2), pp163-179

Canton, R., Clarke, A., Knight, C. and Ward, D. (1996) *Training for Work with Mentally Disordered Offenders: Setting the context*. (Report to the Home Office), Leicester: Dept. of Social and Community Studies, De Montfort University

Cress-Welsing, F. (1991) *ISIS Papers*. Chicago: Third World Press

Dominelli, L. and McLoed, E. (1989) *Feminist Social Work*. London: Macmillan

Douglas, T. (1993) *A Theory of Groupwork Practice*. London: Macmillan

Dyson, S. and Harrison, M. (1998) Black community members as researchers: Two projects compared. in M. Levalette, L. Penketh and C. Jones (eds) *Anti-Racism and Social Welfare*. Aldershot: Ashgate

Evans, M. (ed) (1994) *The Woman Question*. London: Sage

Fleming, J. (1997) Research in the Context of Human Services in Crises. in R. Adams (ed) *Crisis in the Human Services: National and international issues*. Kingston upon Hull: University of Lincolnshire and Humberside

Fleming, J., Harrison, M., Perry, A., Purdey, D. and Ward, D. (1983)

Action speaks louder than words. *Youth and Policy*, 10(3), pp.16-19

Fleming, J., Harrison, M. and Ward, D. (1998) Social Action can be an Empowering Process. *Youth and Policy*, 60, pp.46-62

Fleming, J., Harrison, M. and Ward, D. (forthcoming) *Research as Empowerment: The social action approach.* Aldershot: Ashgate

Fleming, J. and Keenan, E. (1998) *Youth on the Margins in Northern Ireland, England and Ukraine.* Leicester: Centre for Social Action: De Montfort University

Foucault, M. (1980) *Power, Knowledge: Selected Interviews and Other Writings.* New York: Pantheon

Freire, P (1972) *Pedagogy of the Oppressed.* Harmondsworth: Penguin

Giddens, A (1984) *The Constitution of Society.* Cambridge: Polity Press

Giddens, A. (1998) *The Third Way.* Cambridge: Polity Press

Gilroy, P. (1987) *There Ain't No Black in the Union Jack.* London: Hutchinson

Harrison, M., Perry, A. and Ward, D. (1981) Letting the young set the agenda. Community Care, 3rd December, pp.20-21

hooks, bel. (1992) *Ain't I a Woman.* London: Pluto Press

Hudson, A. (1989) Changing perspectives: Feminism, gender and social work. in M. Langan and P. Lee *Radical Social Work Today.* London: Unwin Hyman

Jakobsson, G. (ed) (1995) *Social Work in an International Perspective.* Helsinki: Helsinki University Press

James, T. (1997) Empowerment through social change. *Bridges*, Summer, pp.6-7

Kurland, R. and Salmon, R. (1993) Groupwork versus Casework in a Group. *Groupwork*, 6, 1, pp.5-16

Langan, M. and Day, L. (eds) (1992) *Women, Oppression and Social Work.* London: Routledge

Layder, D. (1994) *Understanding Social Theory.* London: Sage

Lee, J. (1994) *The Empowerment Approach to Social Work Practice.* New York: Columbia University Press

Mistry, T. (1989) Establishing a feminist model of groupwork in the probation service. *Groupwork*, 2, 2, pp.145-158

Mullender, A. and Ward, D. (1991) *Self-Directed Groupwork: Users take action for empowerment.* London: Whiting and Birch

Mullender, A. and Ward, D. (1992) En groupe l'union fait la force. in J. Lindsay (ed) *Textes de Base sur le Modèle de Groupe Autogéré.* Quebec:

École de Service Social, Université Laval.

Mullender, A. and Ward, D. (1996) *Self-Directed Groupwork: Users take action for empowerment.* (translated into Ukrainian), Amsterdam and Kyiv: TACIS/Geneva Initiative

Muldoon, R. (1994/5) The demystification of social action groupwork principles. *Social Action,* 2, 3, pp.9-10

Oliver, M. (1992) Changing the social relations of research production. *Disability, Handicap and Society,* 7, 2, pp.101-114

Page, R. (1992) 'Empowerment, oppression and beyond: A coherent strategy? A reply to Mullender and Ward (CSP Issue 32). *Critical Social Policy,* 35, pp.89-92

Payne, M. (1997) *Modern Social Work Theory.* (2nd Ed) London: Macmillan

Shapiro, B. (1991) Social action, the group and society. *Social Work with Groups,* 14, 3/4, pp.7-22

Staub-Bernasconi, S. (1991) Social action, empowerment and social work: An integrative theoretical framework for social work and social work with groups. *Social Work with Groups,* 14, 3/4, pp.35-51

Treu, H-E., Salustowicz, P., Oldenburg, E., Offe, H. and Neuser, H. (eds.) *Theorie und Praxis der Bekämpfung der Langzeitarbeitslosigkeit in der EG.* Weinheim, Germany: Deutscher Studien Verlag

Vinik, A. and Levin, M. (eds) (1991) *Social Action in Groupwork. (Social Work with Groups,* special issue,14, 3/4). Binghampton, NY: Haworth Press

Ward. D, (1979) Working with young people: The way forward. *Probation Journal,* 26, 1, pp.2-9

Ward, D. (1981) The Chaplefield intermediate treatment project. in R. Adams, S. Allard, J. Baldwin and J/ Thomas (eds) *A Measure of Diversion.* Leicester: National Youth Bureau

Ward, D. (ed) (1982) *Give 'em a Break: Social action by young people at risk and in trouble.* Leicester: National Youth Bureau

Ward, D. (ed) (1989) *Social Action Training Pack.* Nottingham: Centre for Social Action, University of Nottingham

Ward, D. (ed) (1996/7) *Groupwork and Research (Groupwork,* special issue, 9, 2)., London: Whiting and Birch

Ward, D. (1998) Groupwork. in R. Adams, L. Dominelli and M. Payne *Social Work: Themes, issues and critical debates,* London: Macmillan

Wright Mills, C. (1970) *The Sociological Imagination.* Harmondsworth: Penguin.

The contributors

Liz Dixon is Senior Lecturer in Criminal Justice Studies at the University of Hertfordshire, and a Probation Officer with the Inner London Probation Service

Mark Doel is Professor of Social Work and RNIB Rehabilitation Studies at the University of Central England

Jacky Drysdale is Lecturer in Social Work at the University of Wales, Bangor

Linda Finlay is Associate Lecturer in Social Psychology with the Open University

Pam Firth is Senior Social Worker/Head of Family Support at the Isabel Hospice, Welwyn Garden City

Mark Harrison is Director of the Centre for Social Action, De Montfort University, Leicester

Louis B Levy is Acting Director of Health First in Southeast London

Oded Manor is Principal Lecturer in Social Work in the School of Social Science, Middlesex University

Lynne Muir is Course Director, MA in Community Based Learning at the Centre for Education development, Coventry

Rod Purcell is Lecturer in Community Development and Adult Education at the University of Glasgow

Ellen E Reverand is Senior Manager (Learning and Professional Development) with Health First in Southeast London

John Rowan is a Group and Individual Psychotherapist

Catherine Sawdon is a Training Officer with Wakefield Social Services

Marion Silverlock is an Education and Training Consultant based in Somerset

Professor Dave Ward is Head of the Dept of Social and Community Studies, De Montfort University., Leicester